Racing with Aloha

Endorsements

The adventures of Fred are absolutely incredible. Having known Fred and grown up with his kids, I would always hear amazing stories about him. By his humble demeanor, you would never know the life accomplishments he had achieved. I remember my parents had a photograph of when he rode the biggest wave ever at Ho'okipa. The waves were massive, and unlike in today's modern era, there was no safety net. You were on your own, solely relying on yourself and your skills. Still, to this day, I have never seen a spot—or anywhere on Maui's north shore—so big. Reading and learning about what Maui was like between the 1950s and the 1980s is like going back in a time machine. Before I only had questions; now I can imagine I am there. From being one of the best swimmers on the planet to becoming the fastest man on a windsurfer and so much more, I am honored to know someone as humble and inspiring as Fred Haywood.

– Kai Lenny, KaiWatermanLenny.com
professional ocean athlete

Fred and I go back many years. I can remember the swim meet after we both won our first national championship races in Dallas, Texas, in 1967. It was an exciting time for both Fred and me. The two of us were at the San Leandro swim meet at the beginning of the summer season. We were going to swim in an exhibition four-hundred-meter freestyle race with the world record holder, Don Schollander. Fred asked me how I was going to swim the race. I told him I was going to swim eight laps and get out and drive us both back home to Santa Clara forty-five minutes away. That is what I did, but I would swim the four-hundred-meter freestyle in a new world record of 4:10:00 and break the world record of Schollander by two and a half seconds.

Fred was there to break the news to my father when we arrived back home. Since Fred had such an impression of my dad, this was something he couldn't wait to tell. This was my first world record, and Fred and I were together for this great experience. Fred was right at my side in those early years, as I was his. We have remained friends since then. We are here to celebrate Fred, and that is what I want to do. I know how humble you have always been. It is a great quality of yours. Through the passage of time, none of us could forget how you have touched so many people and so many lives. You are a beacon of light that guides every person you meet in the world. The love you gave us through your sports adventures is the story you needed to tell. It is an exciting and inspiring one for everyone to enjoy. Fred, you have been back in Maui for many years, but we still have your great stories and memories, the good you did and the dreams you had. There is a single enduring image I always have of you—the image of a man smiling broadly, ready for what storms may come. Always carrying on toward some new and wondrous place just beyond the horizon, for that last biggest wave to ride, the last fastest windsurfing run, or the last swim meet we swam in together. Fred, as a life that has achieved so much and been such a shining example to so many and to everyone who knows you…we love you.

– **Mark Spitz**, nine-time Olympic gold medalist

By the time I got to Maui in 1985, it was a windsurfing Mecca, and Fred Haywood was a legend in the sport. It was my first year on the Neil Pryde team as a World Cup rider. A photograph hanging on the wall of an apartment I rented showed Fred sailing at Ho'okipa. You could only see the top of his sail through a massive wave exploding behind him. The caption said "Aloha and Welcome to Maui!" I was born in Stockholm where I grew up sailing on inland lakes, so I was impressed. When I got to meet Fred in person, I was struck by his generosity in sharing his knowledge that would help my professional windsurfing career. He knew how to make an individual sport feel like a team sport. At Fuertaventura, I got to hang with the "titans" of the sport: Fred Haywood and Laird Hamilton. I remember feeling very small at the time, next to them. But that meeting opened doors for me. Fred has always been an inspiration for me—after all these years, I still consider him a great friend.

                    – **Anders Bringdal**, professional windsurfer

One day I was surfing at Paukukalo on a decent size day. I saw this guy dropping in on some good-sized lefts, riding them very well backside. A friend of mine said, "That's Big-Wave Fred." We became friends when I started building windsurfing boards for Sailboards Maui in 1981. I made the board Fred took to Weymouth. He made windsurfing history when he broke the thirty-knot barrier on it. Because I had made that board, I was able to tag along on his coattails to successes of my own, which continue to this day. They are directly related to my friendship and professional relationship with Fred and his successes. But more important to me is what Fred had meant to me personally as a friend. He has helped me out simply because he cares, with no other agenda and no expectations of anything in return. That's the Fred Haywood who many people here on Maui know the same way I do.

                    – **Jimmy Lewis**, JimmyLewis.com world class water boards

The Great Briny runs in Fred's veins. What I loved most was understanding that beyond the Olympic trials in Long Beach, he hardly missed a beat and went after "What's Next" with no fear or misgivings about the uniqueness of his journey. Fred had ten more Long Beaches ... and aced every one of them, taking for his prize perfect, vibrant, and profound memories of what he convincingly showed to be the purpose of drawing breath: enjoying the experience. You have done a far better job at that than anyone else I know. That comes through with great energy and joy. Thank you for writing it down.

— **John Ferris**, American competition swimmer
and Olympic medalist

What an incredible life adventure! I was fascinated with one challenge after another, and Fred didn't skip a beat. I found his history of growing up on Maui intriguing and his relationship with his father heartwarming. This will be a good read for anyone, water person or not.

— **Larry Gilbert**, Gilbert & Associates Advertising, Maui

Racing with Aloha shares Fred Haywood's rise from "Fred Who" to becoming the fastest backstroker in America at age seventeen and the fastest windsurfer in the world in 1983, a title he held for two years. He vividly describes growing up on the magical island of Maui in his formative years and the values he learned from his parents of working hard, setting goals, determination, and gratitude. This book is filled with humor, inspiration, humility and sincerity that will be enjoyed by all ages.

— **Joanie Madsen**, former elementary school teacher and
librarian at the Haleakalā Waldorf School

From the water to real estate, Fred has attracted many coaches and mentors. He followed their guidance very closely and has produced incredible results. He has offered me the same mentorship, and it changed my life forever. Fred Haywood has been the single most influential person on my 36-year real estate career on the Valley Isle. Together we opened an international real estate franchise in the mid-nineties that is still thriving. I hope you will enjoy Fred's story as much as I have. The adventures continue as he shares his aloha with the world.

— **Dano Sayles**, Maui realtor

When you grow up in a family of five children—four of them active boys—you recall a blur and a few highlights. Fred always took the time to assess the situation and then would focus on his course of action. When he decided he liked peanut butter and jelly sandwiches, that was all he ate for several weeks. At an early age, he would collect coupons from the supermarket for the Thanksgiving turkey drawings (often going through the line twice in one day), arrange them all in order on a piece of cardboard, and stand up front when the numbers were read. Imagine a preteen boy standing in the front with all the adults. I recall him winning several turkeys on different occasions and carrying them to our home across the street. In the early seventies, when there was a gas shortage, he walked the lines at the service station handing out pens printed with his real estate business number. All this distilled into a perspective of letting things come and go without getting ruffled and continuing to move forward at whatever he decided to do. The attitude has served him well.

— **Guy Haywood**, Maui attorney

I met Fred around 1982 through Barry Spanier and Geoffrey Bourne of Maui Sails, who became the Neil Pryde Design Centre. These were pivotal years – windsurfing was rapidly evolving from recreation into a technical action sport, and the equipment had to keep up. This development was led by the Hawaiian sailors, mostly on Maui, and the trends that Maui set in motion impacted the world windsurfing market. These were also important years for Neil Pryde as we strove to convert from a mass producer of basic windsurfing sails to a world-leading brand with the most desirable products.

Fred Haywood was the perfect ambassador to spread this message: a superb athlete and windsurfing legend from the place where everything was happening. Fred was not only a brilliant sailor but an incredible personality who engendered respect everywhere he sailed.

When we met, Fred was already famous as a powerful wave sailor riding the biggest waves. He was focused on becoming the fastest man on the water to break thirty knots on a windsurfer. This goal was at the time a magical number that was attracting sailors everywhere; it was the four-minute mile of sailing, an objective still out of reach then, too.

Neil Pryde provided the resources that enabled Fred to work with Barry Spanier to create the sail and rig and take Fred to England, where he cracked thirty knots on a Neil Pryde sail. This achievement underpinned the Neil Pryde brand's marketing that spread our market worldwide, becoming the world leader in windsurfing equipment, the world's fastest sails. I remain forever grateful for Fred's contribution to the growth and reputation of the Neil Pryde brand.

– **Neil Pryde**, windsurf sail developer

As Stanford's swim coach in 1968, I was fortunate to have Fred choose Stanford as his university and swimming future. In his three varsity years, Fred won the one-hundred and two-hundred backstroke events each year in the Pac 8 Conference championships. In his first varsity year, he won the NCAA championship in the one-hundred back, beating Indiana's Charlie Hickcox, who was trying to complete his collegiate dominance in the backstroke events. Fred also placed fourth in the two-hundred back and led our four-hundred medley relay to a second-place finish. At the 1970 NCAA championships, Fred led our four-hundred medley relay to victory, setting a new NCAA record while scoring in the one-hundred and two-hundred backstroke and being a part of our four-hundred free relay. In his senior year, Fred joined Olympians Brian Job and John Ferris and freestyler Martin Pedley to win the NCAA championship in the four-hundred medley relay while placing in both backstroke events and being part of our four-hundred free relay. He will always be remembered as one of Stanford's great swimmers.

– **Jim Gaughran**, Stanford University swimming coach, 1960 to 1980

More than fifty-five years ago, I met Fred on the pool deck of Santa Clara Swim Club, coached by George Haines, the greatest coach in the world. George attracted the elite swimmers of the day. Quickly, Fred developed into a national champion. We both got lucky and entered Stanford, where he continued his national success. Later, he became a sailboard and business champion. Today, Fred and I remain something deeper than wonderful old friends. Fred's story is quite remarkable. This book is the story of Fred's inner self, not athletics. What makes a champion in life? How does a man grasp a love of living and aloha? Why does a man have a desire for excellence and vision with so many endeavors? I am blessed to be part of this journey.

– **Rick Eagleston**, competitive swimmer and athletic trainer, Stanford University

Fred and I were teammates and roommates at Stanford. He pretty much came out of nowhere to become a national champion in the backstroke events. The story about upsetting Charlie Hickox is precious, as Charlie had not been beaten in NCAA competition and was not known to be humble. Fred was not only a great swimmer but also a great team leader—he was team captain for our junior and senior years. The sections in this book on his windsurfing career provide interesting insights into Fred's role in creating an entirely new sport. *Racing with Aloha* is a great read for anyone interested in competitive swimming, windsurfing, and Maui life!

– **Bert Mason**, competitive swimmer, Stanford University

In the early seventies, Fred, his brother Jimbo, and I lived together in their old family home on Maui, hidden in the jungle where Hana Highway turns to become Ka'ahumanu Ave. We lived to surf the biggest waves we could find. Maybe it was our mutual birthday or just similar personalities, but Fred and I became life-long friends. My brother had been bringing me out to Bali since the end of high school, and the only person I wanted to share the experience with was Fred. Soon, he joined my brother and me as we ran down the narrow cactus-lined pathways to the isolated surf break off the cliffs of Uluwatu. We had the world-class waves to ourselves back then. I got into hang gliding for several years, and it was Fred who pointed me in a new direction that he thought might be safer—windsurfing. In a short time, he had me follow-ing him across the channels to Molokai or Lanai. Fred was always willing to go big, whether it was distance or speed. But more than athletic adventures, he has always been a reservoir of humor and humility. I've been awed by his willingness to share his insights with the concept of friendship that keeps us slingshotting each other through life and maintaining stoke.

— **Bill Boyum**, surfer, author

We had big fun on the water and land with all kinds of capers, not realizing what we had and how special it was. The north shore of Maui was a classic, small, insular community. We were able to start something that blossomed into a full-on revolution for the sport of windsurfing and Maui's north shore. And we had an awe-some time doing it!

— **Bill King**, Maui builder

Wow! All the stuff I never knew is in these pages. As a forty-year resident of Maui, getting to have a real feel for the ol' kine days was the best part for me, a trip back into a wonderful time of barefoot school days and life in and around the ocean. The details of what we accomplished together, chasing wind and speed, ring so true. Through Fred's skill, I got to experience a life-long dream of being involved with the scientific sailing of a speed contest and then being the ones to set a new world record! And we have been the closest friends ever since. Fun. We had it, and more. Aloha.

— **Barry Spanier**, MauiSails.com sail designer

Maui is forever changing. Fred grew up on Maui, and he has documented a historical perspective of a lifestyle that once was. His story captures the beauty and experiences of life on Maui, which is the essence of aloha.

— **Kim von Tempsky**, retired Maui marketing executive

I first met Fred in the real estate business when he gave me my first big break by aligning his sales team with my mortgage company. His Love Life, Live Maui philosophy has been an inspiration to my career and life. He lives by example—whether he is charging big waves or big real estate deals, he says it's all about the stoke. Everyone should be so lucky to find a friend they can enjoy succeeding in business and life with. We are friends for life.

— **Steven Mangum**, Maui mortgage banker

In *Racing With Aloha*, Fred has woven a fascinating life story that chronicles his youth with the excitement that he experienced in the world of swimming, surfing, and professional windsurfing. His tale reveals the passions of one who thrived, going beyond the limits of what was thought humanly possible, setting multiple world records, while also "living Maui" and sharing the kindness, love, and joy that comes from experiencing a wholesome life on a blessed tropical island.

—**Robert Masters**, Emmy Award-winning filmmaker

Fred was the ring leader who dangled the carrot of desire over our visions of sun-drenched ocean and Maui sand. We followed Fred's beckoning wave to an inspired, golden era of our salad days. Sweet memories of love, fun, adventure, and abounding beauty are captured in *Racing with Aloha*.

– **Mary Jo Masters**, award-winning film producer

Fred had a board shaper named Jimmy Lewis and a sailmaker named Barry Spanier. He asked me to make the hardware to attach Barry's sails to Jimmy's custom boards. Fred wanted a boom made very wide with a custom shape that no one ever thought of. He wanted to position his body farther away from his sail for leverage and to keep a smooth airflow on his sail. And, of course, he wanted to go fast. So we worked together to make his gear at my little shop. It was a success, and he broke the world speed record at Weymouth, England. Fred helped me get all the best and fastest sailors. Because of Fred, I started a new windsurfing company called Hawaiian Pro Line. Over the years, I worked with all the top professionals in the world of windsurfing world. But I never had a rider who was so helpful and pushed so hard to have the tools he needed for his passion as Fred Haywood.

– **Keith Baxter**, Baxter Charters

As a family man, business leader, and waterman, Fred has always been an inspiration and mentor. He is always willing to share his valuable wisdom and takes a genuine interest in helping others succeed. Family first, positive thinking, and having gratitude with lots of aloha have proven to be my key tools to success, thanks to Fred.

– **Bradley Newton**, surfer, world traveler, entrepreneur

Way back in 1984, I was somewhat accomplished at surfing and had started windsurfing when I ran across Fred's picture in *Windsurf* magazine. He was riding a wave that was easily fifty feet on the face. Thinking I'd like to do that, I packed up and moved to Maui. From the inspiration of that photo, my life had changed. After working at Sailboards Maui for a few years (a company he founded with his friends), I was fortunate to take over the shop and raise my family in Haiku, Maui. Thanks, Fred, for thirty-five years of friendship and inspiration!

— **Dave Mel**, owner at Sailboards Maui

Racing with Aloha

AN *Inspiring* JOURNEY
FROM HUMBLE BAREFOOT MAUI BOY TO
Champion IN THE WATER

FRED HAYWOOD

FOREWORD BY
Laird Hamilton

NEW YORK

LONDON • NASHVILLE • MELBOURNE • VANCOUVER

Racing with Aloha

An Inspiring Journey from Humble Barefoot Maui Boy to Champion in the Water

Published in New York, New York, by Morgan James Publishing. Morgan James is a trademark of Morgan James, LLC. www.MorganJamesPublishing.com

Excerpt reprinted courtesy of SPORTS ILLUSTRATED: "The Times Came for Two Teens" by Kim Chapin, April 17, 1967. Copyright © 1967. ABG-SI LLC. All rights reserved.

ISBN 9781631953712 paperback
ISBN 9781631953729 ebook
Library of Congress Control Number: 2020948262

Cover and Interior Design by:
Chris Treccani
www.3dogcreative.net

Cover Photo Credit:
Arnaud de Rosnay, courtesy of Jenna de Buretel

Morgan James is a proud partner of Habitat for Humanity Peninsula and Greater Williamsburg. Partners in building since 2006.

Get involved today! Visit
MorganJamesPublishing.com/giving-back

For

Debbie Davis
The Haywood *Ohana*
Skyler Haywood, Meryl Haywood, and Evan Haywood

Table of Contents

Foreword

The Ambassador of Aloha

have found there are two kinds of people: competitive people and creative people. Competitive people are fulfilled by beating others, and creative people are fulfilled by accomplishing things.

Fred Haywood and I both grew up in Hawaii, influenced by the tropical environment of the Hawaiian Islands—at times nurturing and at other times fierce. The formidable ocean drew us irresistibly to her to challenge our abilities at riding her magnificent power. At the same time, the gentle nature of the Hawaiian culture infused us both with the spirit of aloha.

Aloha is a creative, collaborative philosophy. Hawaiians have always favored creativity over competition, curiosity over judgment. They aren't very concerned with keeping a secret that might give them an edge over the other guy. They are more curious about how they can partner with others, working in a community to offer input, listen, and come up with ideas in the interest of the whole. Success is greater among people who work with each other rather than against each other.

When you live in Hawaii for most of your life as I have, embodying the spirit of aloha, you value collaboration and camaraderie over competition. And that is the essence of Fred Haywood. That is what Fred and I have in common: we enjoy connecting with and helping people. In fact, I may have learned this from Fred one day in 1983 on a challenging windsurfing run on Kauai.

The sport was becoming popular, and I was new to it compared to Fred. The run from Tunnels to Hanalei Bay was challenging, winds were maybe fifty knots, and we were climbing twenty-foot whitewater waves—impossible on a surfboard, but not on a windsurfer. I've always been a bit of an adventurer on the water, and this day was no different. I was dancing maybe just a little too high on the waves (some thirty feet in the air?) when Fred summoned me down. If I had broken down, Fred would never have been able to find me in the whitewater. This day was another lesson in my ocean life about functioning within the limits of your skillset and your equipment. My career has been a series of trying to work within and yet push the limits with respect and calculation. It is truly the only way to operate year after year.

The next day I tried the same trick in calmer waters, and I broke the fin off my board. That accident could have been life-threatening the day before. I was young and full of testosterone. Fred knew exactly when to rein me in, and he only did it when he knew it would help me be better on the water.

That run to Hanalei was the beginning of many adventures between Fred and myself, building a lifelong bond of love and respect.

Three years later, at a windsurfing contest in France, Fred challenged me to outrace the French champion, Pascal Maka. The French were crazy about windsurfing, and they were even crazier for Pascal. Fred and Pascal had tossed records back and forth for a few years in what Fred considered a friendly rivalry. It did feel a bit more serious for Pascal.

On the last day of the competition, I was in third place when the winds died. Pascal was in first, and it looked like the contest was over. Suddenly, the weather changed. The officials, in typical French style, spontaneously decided to open the course again. Everybody scrambled to the start line to get some runs in. I don't know if I had a problem with my rig or if Fred knew his would be a little faster.

"Here, try my rig," he said. "Go out there and beat Pascal!"

Fortunately, on this day, I did.

After my third run, I broke a European speed record. I was surprised and thrilled! Not to mention it may have been made a little sweeter by beating Pascal on his home turf. Best of all—I earned my first sponsorship with Neil Pryde Sails, the largest sail builder in the world. It was a Cinderella story, and Fred made it happen for me. He was willing to give up the chance to beat his perennial adversary, and he gave me his equipment to attempt it myself.

That experience was one of many pivotal points in my career as a waterman. Winning that event and getting sponsorship contributed to my going on and with a crew to pioneering tow-in surfing at Jaws on Maui. This way of approaching water sports contributed to how I would approach riding waves and a lot of other innovations I have been fortunate to be a part of.

I have Fred to thank—for the gear that day, for the encouragement, for introducing me to Neil Pryde, and for his willingness to step back and let me have a shot at the win.

That is the spirit of aloha. Fred has always been an ambassador of aloha. I've traveled with him all over the world, and I have seen him share it with everyone, from young kids like me, filled with testosterone, to experienced water athletes. They never threatened his essential nature or competitive urge. "Sometimes you'll be faster; sometimes I will be," Fred says. He doesn't hold back on helping people.

Because when you listen, when you live in Hawaii, when you are immersed in the ocean's enormous power, you realize no one's a threat. That most of the time, we all need each other to get through life with grace. This understanding is what Fred has mastered and has modeled. And this is what you will read in *Racing with Aloha*.

I'm glad Fred is sharing his story. This book entertains, informs, and inspires. There are heroes amongst us, and Fred is one of mine.

Laird Hamilton
Waterman, Innovator, Pioneer, Health & Fitness Leader

A Note by Mike Waltze
On Ocean Icons and Innovations

'll never forget my first encounter with Fred. I had no money, and I was teaching windsurfing on the beach at the Sheraton Ka'anapali on Maui for room and board. Every day, I would see this guy sitting in a beach chair under a tree reading a book. One morning, I was walking down from the hotel to set up for my lessons when I saw that same guy, without asking, dragging one of my sailboards into the water. I was a bit shocked because up until then we hadn't met. And I told him so. Picture it: I'm a scrawny, short eighteen-year-old scolding this huge guy ten years older for not asking first.

Well, within an hour, I had given Fred a proper windsurfing lesson. We discovered he was a natural. The friendship that followed has lasted a lifetime, and no wonder.

Two weeks after that first windsurfing lesson, Fred cosigned a loan for me so I could quit my job, buy a car, move to the north shore, and sail Ho'okipa every day. Before long, he borrowed money from his dad so he could do the same.

I honestly believe had I not met Fred that day, my life would have been very different. Many people's lives may have been very different.

The innovation, the creativity, the camaraderie, the smiles, the laughter, the sun, the waves, the fear, the joy... we launched an era of icons and innovations on the water. With Matt Schweitzer, Laird Hamilton, Mark Angulo, Dave Kalama, Pete Cabrinha, Robbie Naish, Rush Randall, Brett Lickle, and others, we forged friendships, engraved memories, and above all, had so much fun on the ocean.

Without Fred's enthusiasm and belief in windsurfing, I'm convinced that Maui would never have become the sport's Mecca. Because of Fred, most of his hang-gliding and surfer friends, including Gerry Lopez, came to this crazy sport that everyone could do when Maui was too windy for anything else. We had enough local business to open the first windsurfing shop—Sailboards Maui—and within a year, we organized the first wave sailing and high-speed slalom events at Ho'okipa. That event opened the eyes of many other sailors around the world and put Ho'okipa in the spotlight.

Now with a few handfuls of world-class sailors living on Maui, this dynamic and colorful aspect of the sport in the waves began to dazzle the rest of the world. Then Fred went out and broke the world speed record. Photographers, filmmakers, TV producers, and magazines from dozens of countries flocked to Maui's quiet north shore. Dozens more exceptional athletes followed. Soon every major sailmaker and board manufacturer had a sail loft and shaping room here, and there was no turning back. While working with Maui's local craftsmen, we watched Da Kine, Naish Hawaii, and Jimmy Lewis go from garage hobbies to international corporations.

What started as a passion for just a few people became the epicenter of a worldwide industry. Even after windsurfing began to fade, new sports inspired by our same group of friends would fill the gaps. Kiteboarding, stand-up paddling, tow-in surfing, and foil boarding are, in a sense, all a spinoff from windsurfing. The same core group of windsurfing athletes pioneered each of these sports, and Maui was the epicenter for all of them.

Fred is the most quiet-mannered man I have ever met. I can't recall a time when he raised his voice or a hand, but inside, he's a tiger. Fred Haywood sees something he wants and humbly goes after it. The gratitude I have for him is without words, as he was the catalyst that has bonded me to so many of the amazing friends that you will read about in this book. I wonder what would have happened—or not happened—had I not met Fred.

Every day was an adventure, and every adventure led to another—which is exactly how life should be lived. Life is a series of stories, and this era of watersports stories showcases, without a doubt, some of the best.

Ho'okipa

had just set the windsurfing world speed record in 1983, breaking the thirty-knot barrier in Weymouth, England, but that's not how I made my name in the sport. My fame came on a day when I was surfing alone, thanks to an eccentric and very wealthy fellow windsurfer and cover photographer for such magazines as *Vogue* and *Life*, who showed up to watch me after everyone else had left the beach for the day.

One morning, I was driving along Hana Highway on Maui when I could see Arnaud de Rosnay cruising toward me in his convertible.

"Hey, Fred!" he called.

Waving wildly, he stopped me on the road, and we chatted while our cars idled. In those days on the island, traffic was light, and we could sit there for several minutes without worrying about blocking traffic.

Arnaud was dressed all in white, his long hair blowing in the breeze. Before the end of the year, the dashing and wealthy French baron would disappear, attempting to windsurf across the South China Sea's one-hundred-mile Taiwan Strait. But on this particular blustery spring day in 1984, Arnaud was eager to photograph what he claimed would be the best day to surf the north shore of Maui.

1

"The biggest waves in the world will be coming in at Ho'okipa today. I'll be there at noon with a helicopter to shoot it. Come sail at noon!"

"Yeah, I know," I said to him. "But I'll be there at three. I'm going to sail a really big wave at around four o'clock, maybe four-thirty."

"But I'll have the helicopter there at noon!" Arnaud insisted.

"I've been sailing every day," I told him, "and every day, the big waves have been coming late. The biggest set of the day will come around four. I don't want to sail until it's going to get really big. I think someone is going to ride the biggest wave in the world, and I want to be the one."

It was an exciting time to be surfing on Maui. Matt Schweitzer, Mike Waltze, Pete Cabrinha, Malte and Klaus Simmer, Dave Kalama, Laird Hamilton, Craig Masonville, Robbie Naish, Greg and Alex Aguera, Vince Hogan and I were experimenting and innovating with our boards on the water. We weren't the first to do anything, but we convinced those who were that Maui was the place to push their limits. They came. They pushed. And windsurfing took off, followed by big wave tow-in and paddle-in, stand-up paddling, kite sailing, and foil-boarding. Maui offered the stage that showcased the stars.

I have lived on Maui my whole life. I know the water. I know the waves. I knew Ho'okipa, a beach that offers some of the biggest challenges for board surfing in the world but was pretty much a secret in the early eighties.

I showed up at three o'clock to find David Ezzy, Malte Simmer, Mike Eskimo, and Craig Maisonville there, and so was the helicopter. I stood on the beach to watch Malte Simmer going up to face a wave, making a turn at the top, and coming back down.

The waves were huge, indeed. The faces were maybe forty or fifty feet—the hugest I had ever seen at Ho'okipa. I started to second-guess myself. I wondered if I had misjudged the best time to be on the water. I rigged up to sail out on a 5.9-square-meter sail with a seventeen-foot mast—a big rig for my windsurf board, which was a can-opener style.

I tried to sail out, but I had to push over whitewater twice as high as my mast, and a few threw me back. It took me thirty minutes to cover what should have taken me thirty seconds—if I hadn't kept getting blasted by the waves. When I finally got outside, the wind suddenly dropped. It was late. I looked left and right, and I saw nobody. The helicopter was gone. Everyone had gone in.

"Okay. Oh, well," I said to myself. I hadn't come for the helicopter. I just wanted to surf the world's biggest wave that day.

And then I did.

I waited for what seemed like forever for that wave. It wouldn't come through. I took a few, but the waves weren't that big. I kicked out to look for it.

And then I saw out in the distance, a mile or two away, a wave that was standing some twenty feet above the others. That was it. This was the tide change. By the time the wave caught me, I was hydroplaning. The wind was turning more offshore now, and I was going almost straight upwind. To drop in, I had to veer off to the right and slide across the wave.

I got to the top and looked down—I must have been six stories high. I took the power in my hands, and I zipped down the face. I ran out on the flat, trying to get in front of it. I didn't know when it would break.

All of a sudden, the lip of that wave came over and crashed right on my tail block. I almost ditched my rig, but I held on by my fingertips. It didn't hit me. There was whitewater all around me. I hung on my boom. A moment later, I caught a blast of wind from the collapsing wave and started sailing. It took me back to land and pushed me right up to the dirt bank at the back of the beach.

I lay there, taking it all in.

I did it, I thought. And then, as if I had spoken out loud…

"You did it!" I heard someone holler. "Fred! YOU DID IT! You surfed the biggest wave in the world!"

It was Arnaud. I looked up to see him running toward me through the sand with a camera bouncing around his neck. Everyone else had left. But not Arnaud. Arnaud was a real pro, both on the water and behind the lens. He would never miss the wave—or the shot.

"I got it!" he exclaimed. "I shot a whole roll of film on one wave. You are going to be famous! These pictures will make you even more famous than breaking the world record!"

Arnaud was right. I made all the top trade magazines. But the one that put me on the map was *Life* magazine. In 1984, *Life* was widely admired by a broad general audience for its photojournalism.

Arnaud's photos won me a windsurfing sponsorship, launching my professional career in speed sailing and earning me sponsorships for nearly a decade. Not bad for a boy who grew up on the beaches of Maui and went to grade school barefoot.

My love of the water started when I was baptized, figuratively speaking, in Kahului Harbor at the age of seven.

My Never-Ending Summer

was seven years old when my dad taught me the meaning of "sink or swim."

Maui was my personal paradise in the mid-1950s. We lived on the beach in Kahului in a neighborhood of only ten or twelve families. Of those families that had kids, most of them were boys, so my three brothers and I never lacked for pals to run with. In fact, as with most kids of my generation, we played outside all day. Our moms shooed us out after breakfast and didn't want us back in the house until they called us for dinner.

One Saturday afternoon, I was sitting on our back lanai eating peanut butter sandwiches and drinking milk with my older brothers, Guy and Jimbo. It was winter, which in Hawaii meant the temperature dropped into the seventies and the breeze picked up by midday.

Dad stepped out from the kitchen, letting the screen door slam behind him. If one of us kids had done that, we would have heard Mom holler for sure. But Dad could do no wrong, of course, in Mom's opinion.

"Come on, Fred," he said. "I need your help. Let's go down to the boat."

I don't recall why he needed me. All I remember is my delight at being asked. My older brothers were sitting right there, and he could have picked either of them. Dad was a busy doctor, and time for just the two of us was rare. I shoved the rest of the sandwich into my mouth and gulped my drink to wash it down.

Dad was halfway to his pickup truck, and I tore after him, barefoot. (We never wore shoes except to church—not even to school!) I climbed into the cab, and Dad drove us to Pier 1 in Kahului Harbor a few minutes from our house. I jumped out, ran along the dock that stretched out into the harbor, trotted down to our boat, and climbed aboard.

The boat was a fishing boat built by his good friend Glen Fredholm and named, appropriately, *Docsout*.

Dad puttered around with the lines, making sure we were secure to the dock. Then he started up the motor and listened. He messed around with some other stuff—I don't remember what—until he remembered he had left something in the back of the truck.

"Fred, I'll be back. I'm going to get the water hose to wash down the boat. You stay here in the stern. Okay, buddy?"

I nodded and promptly forgot his instruction. Wandering around the cockpit, I relished my first time alone on it and pretended I was the captain, navigating to Molokai. When Dad came back, I was peering out from the bow, in search of the neighbor island.

He walked up to me, growling, "I thought I told you to stay in the stern!"

"Oh, Dad, don't worry," I said proudly and just a bit cavalierly, as any seven-year-old water rat might. "I can swim!"

The next thing I knew, I was in the water.

Dad had just straight-armed me in the chest, flipping me back into the harbor. I quickly popped up, spluttering more from surprise than fear.

"You stay in there and think about how well you can swim!" he ordered.

I treaded water until I thought I might sink, while Dad hooked up the hose to wash the boat. Finally, he waved at me to climb up.

I grabbed onto a slimy rope covered in who-knows-what-spikey, biting creatures that grow in ocean water, and, with no help whatsoever, scrambled my way up to the boat deck. I stood there, shocked and shivering in the cool ocean air.

Dad handed me one of his old work shirts to cover up my wet clothes. I must have looked like a drowned rat with the shirttail and the long sleeves hanging to my ankles. He never said another word about my disobedience. Lesson learned. I did my best from then on not to cross him.

I wasn't born in the water, but I grew up in it. The beach was twenty feet from our backyard. I felt like I spent more of my waking hours in the ocean than on land. Growing up on Maui in the 1950s felt like every day was summer vacation.

There were five of us kids. Anne was the oldest. Guy was three years older than me, Jim a year ahead, and Bill was three years younger. We boys tended to run in a pack. I was eager to follow my older brothers into the water, even as a toddler. Mom would take the time to teach us to swim, helping the weaker swimmer in the water. Or she would sit in a beach chair while we played in the sand. We started body surfing first, then graduated to those old-fashioned canvas air mattresses with the long tubular air bars. I would paddle out into the harbor on one, and ride the waves back in.

Dad bought us an old yellow twelve-foot board made of balsa wood. (It would be years before we would see a foam surfboard.) We called it the "Banana Boat." It was so long that Jimbo, Bill, and I could ride together. The Banana Boat floated well enough, but it was hard to turn. It had a big fin for steering, which we called a skeg back then, glued onto the bottom. The rocker is the bottom curve of the board from the nose to the tail. The Banana Boat's rocker had an extra piece of balsa wood glued to the nose so it could be shaped into a curve. A good rocker helps the board accommodate the curl of a wave, allowing it to glide out onto the flat of the wave easily without "pearling"—a term that describes a nose-diving wipeout resembling pearl divers plunging way below the surface of the water. That was not what we wanted to do!

Kahului Harbor, right out our back door, was our playground, and we had lots of fun surfing in it. In the fifties, the harbor entrance was wider than it is now, allowing us to experience some decent waves. Evidently, the wave activity was too strong for commercial traffic—the Matson container ships, cruise boats, and other visiting vessels—so they dredged the harbor and narrowed the entryway. That spoiled the surf, so we switched to boats for backyard fun.

We had a couple of wooden El Toro sailboats—the small dinghy with a blunt nose and a simple single mast was easy for kids to sail. The wind picked up nicely after ten o'clock. We raced our friends in the harbor on weekends. It was exciting, and we sailed every day we wanted to.

On calm days, we would take out a little rowboat or motorboat, pitch an anchor, and catch fish. We'd catch bonefish, called *o'io* in Hawaiian, in the flats in the center of the harbor. Or we'd go under the pier to catch the prize of the reef, the *papio,* trolling off the back of the boat with shrimp on hooks. Of course, there was nothing better than a couple of papio fried up and paired with some seven-cent cone sushi we picked up at the original free-standing Noda Market in the Kahului Shopping Center.

(Cone sushi is a Japanese treat of sweet seasoned rice in a fried bean curd wrapper.)

We had some decent luck catching o'io and papio in Kahului Harbor, so we decided to aim for larger prey. One evening, we attempted to fashion a shark trap. We attached a weighted cord from an old double-hung window to a glass ball—we had a small collection gathered on early morning beach walks, washed up from Japanese fishing nets. Then we attached a large hook to a wire leader and baited it with a skipjack tuna (*aku*) head we scrounged from a trash can behind the shopping center. We placed our baited hook and lines in the middle of the harbor. Our concept was good but poorly executed.

When my brothers and I woke up the next morning, we ran out to see if we caught anything. We probably did, but there was no sign of our efforts. It never occurred to us to hook the contraption to a buoy to secure our catch. All we could assume was that somewhere in the ocean a shark had scooped up the aku and was trailing our float and lines.

We managed to catch plenty of baby hammerhead sharks from the pier. We proudly took them home to Mom, who had absolutely no intention of feeding them to her family. She never uttered a discouraging word to us, of course, because, well, Mom never said a discouraging word about anything. She just put them in the freezer with what Dad caught deep-sea fishing.

Then there was the day my little brother Bill tried fishing from his bike. He was riding along the pier, searching the water for fish, when he rode right off the end and landed in the water. All he caught was a large gash on his lip.

Eventually, we had surfboards to outfit the five of us. Dad probably received those boards in lieu of payment for services in his medical practice!

Mom would take us around the island on weekends. We would stack all the boards on top of her car and leave early to catch the best waves. The best spots were Honolua Bay, Maalaea, Paukukalo, and Ho'okipa. In those days—the sixties—we often had the ocean to ourselves with maybe a few friends. It was rare to pass other cars carrying surfboards. If we did pass surfers, we would wave and give a thumbs-up or down to indicate the quality of the surf at the nearby beach. This was long before weather maps or beach cameras!

At an early age, we became watermen and weathermen as we learned to track the best surf on the island. Dad taught us to look at the lowest string of clouds to see the angle of the winds. From our home in Kahului, we could look out at the ocean and track the cloud movements to learn where the winds were blowing. The cloud movements would indicate where we would find offshore winds for the best wave forces. We knew conditions. We preferred offshore winds for the best surf.

Ohana

learned to live my life like I rode the ocean waves. Water sports involve harnessing energy from the winds to move over the water. Once I learned the paradox of going with the flow no matter what lay in front of me, I applied this skill to my life. It unfolded easily and almost magically. While he never voiced such a concept, preferring to let me learn by experience, I credit my dad for teaching me this.

I was born on Maui in 1949, two years after my parents, Guy and Anita Haywood, moved with my sister Anne and brother Guy to the island from San Francisco, where Dad was stationed while he was in the Army Medical Corps.

The island was essentially a company town, and most employees—from the laborers to the executives—lived in housing owned by the sugar and pineapple plantations. Each plantation provided housing for their employees, called camps, generally segregated by race—Japanese, Chinese, Filipino, and Portuguese. Each of the major sugar mills—Paia, Puunene, Wailuku, and Lahaina— was owned by different corporations. The medical services for the workers for each mill were separate hospitals or clinics.

Dad had responded to an ad in the *San Francisco Chronicle* to work as a doctor for the Hawaiian Commercial & Sugar Plantation (HC&S) for four hundred dollars a month, about half what doctors on the mainland made. HC&S also provided Dad a large two-story, three-bedroom house with an unfinished walk-in attic in a little neighborhood of less than a dozen homes. It was a typical plantation-style design of single-wall wood construction and a shingle roof, deep overhangs, large windows to let in the trade winds, shaded by cooling tropical vegetation.

An outdoorsman when he lived in Montana, Dad was eager to try his hand at watersports. He hustled a house on the beach of Kahului Harbor (and a place to dock a boat as part of the deal), claiming the need for proximity to any sick laborers who might arrive from overseas and need prompt medical care.

In addition to working in the hospital, Dad made house calls in the plantation camps. He carried a big black bag—the classic doctor's bag that opened from the top to expose needles, medications, and other tools of his trade. His patients paid him a dollar a home visit.

Sometimes Dad would take me to the hospital emergency room to see accident victims. He wanted me to see what could happen if I was not careful. I found it pretty pitiful. I had a sensitive physical disposition; I can remember backing out of the room into the hallway of the hospital, lying on the floor, and putting my feet up on the wall so I wouldn't faint. Fainting was a sensation I would become all too familiar with ten years later in my championship swimming career, eventually ending it.

Dad didn't really know how to express his affection for us kids. He wasn't good at it. But he gave us a lot of freedom. We had cats and dogs; we had bikes; we had a small cadre of friends from our neighborhood. Like most kids in the fifties, we pretty much ran wild during the day—from the beach to the newly constructed Kahului Shopping Center.

We always made sure Dad had time to let off steam after work. He might be a little grumpy after working all day, so we would go down to the beach. Having to step over our bikes scattered on the sidewalk outside the house always annoyed him. (I'm putting that nicely!) So did coming home to a house full of mayhem. It was safer to come home a bit later than he did. We would let him mellow out first.

Mom would ring a big bell to call us in for dinner. We could hear it a couple of blocks away. Dinner was prime time for five active kids. With brothers, none of us could afford to look away from our plates. We guarded our food carefully. If you didn't, you might find a fork poised to snag a bite.

We frequently had a crowd around the dinner table—friends were always welcome, including girlfriends as we got older. Sometimes we'd pull two tables together to accommodate ten or twelve of us, including friends. Mom would spread a tapa cloth—a traditional material made of beaten bark—across the tables and set a coral display in the middle. We always had a lot of fun and made a big ruckus. But Dad wouldn't allow anyone to brag about themselves. If anyone started spouting off, he would shut them down quickly, and not always kindly. Humility was his most prized character trait, and it is one I have taken seriously and valued all my life.

Dad believed in hands-on learning. He had a fishing boat he named *Haole Sampan*. Hawaiians call white people *haoles* (pronounced "how-lee"), and Sampan referred to an old, dilapidated boat. Dad had plenty of money, but he saw no reason to spend it unnecessarily. When we needed it, money was there, whether it was food on the table or a good education. He quietly provided support for everything we wanted to do.

He put an old Caterpillar engine in that boat and painted the bottom with four coats of fiberglass. At high speed, it might have reached all of five knots. That was good enough for him. It was the difference between owning an old Packard and a sports car. And he knew the difference, too, between a Packard and a sports car. He was happy with it.

One day, he took me to our rowboat on the dock. We used it to take us out to the fishing boat that happened to be moored on an anchor in the harbor.

"Okay," Dad said. "Now, row us out."

I had no idea what to do. He had never shown me. I can remember feeling intimidated and overwhelmed. I don't remember how well I did. I just know I got us there.

That was Dad's teaching moment. I learned more than how to row a boat that day. I learned I could do anything I put my mind to.

If Dad was powerful and demanding, Mom was his counterpart: gentle and forgiving. She personified positivity. To her, "if you can't say something nice, don't say anything at all" was a principle, and far from a cliché. Mom used to play bridge with her girlfriends. I can remember one of them saying Mom was one of the few people she knew who never said anything negative about another person.

If Dad was an active influence in my life, Mom taught me to always look for the good in any situation. In times of conflict, her example serves me still, many decades later, to bypass judgment and go to curiosity.

Mom was our lifeguard when we were on the beach or in the harbor. She chauffeured us around the island in a station wagon piled with a load of surfboards. She carpooled us to school and swim practice. She was essentially our activities director, in addition to keeping house and feeding all of us.

Because we were on the beach every day, we tracked in sand, oblivious to any tasks this would add to her housekeeping. She begged us every night to please wash our feet before we got into bed. It was a small request on her part to make laundry day just a bit easier. I don't think any of us paid attention, and our bedsheets were permanently stained at the bottom.

Fortunately, she had help. When we were younger, a high school girl lived with us during the school year, except on weekends, and helped Mom in exchange for room and board. In the fifties, homes had few conveniences. Mom needed help to get food on the table and keep our clothes clean. Mitsuro Nakamura—we called her Mitzy—was the oldest of six kids, so she had experience in a large family. She lived at Ulupalakua Ranch, where her dad worked. Ulupalakua Ranch was a 40,000-acre cattle ranch on Haleakala, and it would have taken Mitzy an hour and a half in those days to get down the mountain to the high school. Dad drove her to school, and she helped Mom with the chores in the afternoons. Those were the days when clothes had to be ironed and dishes washed by hand. If they went out for the evening, she would stay with us. It was an excellent set-up for everyone.

Later, Rachel Santos spent most of her high school years with us.

Mom needed all the help she could get. Did she create a warm household with comfort food on the table every night? Far from it. Life for Mom was one of survival—and by that I mean keeping four practically feral boys alive to adulthood! Someone was always in the refrigerator or jumping on the couch. Jimbo may have been her biggest challenge. He was full of pranks, like sticking a pair of scissors in an electrical outlet. And then there was the year he pulled the Christmas tree down on himself.

Anne managed to sidestep our raucousness, of course. She didn't play with us boys, and she went off to boarding school on Oahu when she entered the eighth grade. I was only eight. Like in any neighborhood in those days, the neighbors kept us in line. Everybody knew all the kids, especially since there weren't many haole kids in Kahului. The neighborhood was small—maybe just a dozen families—but there was a preponderance of boys. We'd all get together and ride bikes or play cops and robbers. It was a whole bunch of fun, concentrated into just a few years since we boys each went away to boarding school when we reached the eighth grade—in our case to Hawaii Preparatory Academy on the Big Island.

Hui

Maui was in the midst of a significant transition while I was young. World War II had ended. The International Longshore and Warehouse Union succeeded in unionizing the plantation workers, and the sugar and plantation workers commanded higher paychecks. At the same time, the plantations looked for ways to mechanize the work to reduce the rising labor costs commanded by the unions. They also began to phase out the plantation camps in favor of creating opportunities for plantation workers to buy their own homes.

HC&S developed a master plan for a community to be built around Kahului Harbor, called Dream City. Plantation workers would be able to buy homes for under ten thousand dollars.

It would take another twenty-five years for Dream City to be completed, and my brothers and I were delightfully oblivious to any change. Dad still provided medical care for the plantation workers.

We also were oblivious to any sense of racial disparity. There weren't enough people living on Maui in the 1950s—just 35,000—to concern oneself with differences. Dad's colleagues at the Puunene hospital were Chinese and Japanese, as well as white. Some of our friends had grandparents who spoke only Japanese. It was not a surprise to see old Chinese women hobbling through the shopping center on tiny feet that had been bound when they were girls.

Our neighbors were Japanese, the Yorimotos; Chinese, the Wongs; and what we called locals, i.e. Hawaiian, the Akakas. We white kids included our neighbor friends from the Barkley, Gammie, Eggleston, and Gillen families. Their dads were professionals—what one might then have considered "white-collar workers"—with the plantations or the railroad. While the kids in our neighborhood may have been segregated by income from the kids growing up in the camps, none of us saw color. Well, that's not true. Everybody knew what color they were, and everybody got along.

We were called haoles, today considered a disparaging term for Caucasians, but one that never gave us offense then. There was a subtle discrimination between the races, but not like on the mainland. In Hawaii, every ethnic group was treated differently, but there was no single race in the majority, so everyone worked it out.

Today an active sovereignty movement is dedicated to reclaiming the Hawaiian heritage, and rightly so. American missionaries and businessmen dominated life and commerce on the islands for nearly two hundred years, unfortunately subjugating peaceable Hawaiians to second-class status. That is changing now.

I encountered racism as a concept for the first time in a class at Stanford in which black students shared their experiences of being minorities in a white community. I was astounded at the idea that people could experience prejudice because of the color of their skin.

The "locals" throughout Hawaii are committed to sharing the treasured concept of *aloha*—treating others with love and compassion—and other unique Hawaiian teachings and practices. But even today, I do not feel excluded from the Hawaiian culture, nor will I allow myself to be excluded. I was born on Maui, but I don't call myself a Hawaiian. That designation honors those of Polynesian heritage. Nevertheless, I am entitled to claim this island as my home, and I do.

While we kids were aware of everybody's background, as far as I could tell, Mom and Dad were oblivious to ethnic distinctions. House parties were popular social gatherings, and a couple dozen families living in central Maui would gather on a Saturday night at someone's house, kids included. The fare was generally potluck, featuring a range of local and ethnic delicacies from sushi to barbeque. One evening we all went to the Patterson family's house. They lived only five miles up the mountain from Kahului on a few acres on Pulehu Road, but the drive was about half an hour up a narrow gravel road, and a long, tree-lined drive meandering up to the house. There may have been thirty kids there that night, playing outside and eating a potluck picnic, while our parents gathered inside to enjoy cocktails and a nice meal. We hung out with kids whose dads worked for HC&S, Alexander & Baldwin, and Maui Land & Pineapple. The Baldwin name on Maui was considered next to royalty then; the family reigned from the missionary culture of the 1830s to their mid-twentieth-century command of the sugar industry, cattle ranching, and politics. But to us kids, no one was any better than anyone else. They were just our friends.

Mauka to Makai

When I was growing up, 35,000 people were clustered in small, distinct communities scattered across the island. Wailuku, the county seat, is near Kahului, and Waihee is just beyond that. My dad worked at the hospital in Puunene. These towns are in the valley between the volcano of Haleakala—which we just called the mountain—and the West Maui Mountains. Kula is upcountry—a big, undeveloped area on the side of Haleakala known for cattle farms. Paia, a small town on the north shore, was home of the Paia Sugar Mill. Up Baldwin Avenue is Makawao, known as a Portuguese cowboy town. Over to the south is Kihei, a hot desert town of scrappy kiawe trees where no one wanted to go. Driving to Lahaina on the west side of the island was an excursion—a two-hour drive along a partially unpaved road. It was no wonder Mom let us skip church on Sundays to go surfing on that side of the island. Kahakuloa on the northwest side might as well have been as far away as the moon. The drive to the west side of Maui improved when the tunnel opened. But still, if we went around to Ka'anapali for parties, it was a journey.

Every year, we'd get to go to the Maui County Fair. The exhibits in the fairground buildings ranged from cattle to orchids. We loved the carnival rides, even a roller coaster and a Ferris wheel, brought over from Oahu. They even had a stadium with car races.

Folks traveled from all the islands and even the mainland to attend this fun event.

The Kahului Railroad Company delivered sugar on a train from the Kahului yard west to the Wailuku Sugar Mill and east to Spreckelsville, Upper Paia, Hamakuapoko, and Haiku. Sometimes they would have a special day when school kids and the Cub Scouts could ride it. We would go to the train station, and they'd have the engine with an open car with seats in it. We'd all climb in and travel to the Pauwela cannery in Haiku, across the wooden trestle at Maliko Gulch, and back. The gulch dropped a couple hundred feet below the trestle, the highest bridge built on Maui at the time. Riding across the gulch was scary and exciting, so it was a big deal for us kids.

There are maybe a dozen microclimates on Maui, thanks to the valleys, plains, and mountains. The winds blast the west side with hot, dry air. It is pretty chilly year-round upcountry in Kula. Haleakala can be downright cold, even on a summer morning. And the east side of the island is a wet, tropical rainforest. We never had a shortage of outdoor opportunities, whether we wanted to go hiking, camping, swimming, or surfing.

We had fun all over the island, from the beach, the swimming holes, and waterfalls, to trips to Hana and the top of Haleakala, which was a special family excursion. The volcano reaches down twenty-eight thousand feet to the ocean floor, so it is, in fact, a higher mountain than Everest. The top of the dormant volcano is a national park of more than thirty thousand acres, and it is said to hold more endangered species than any other U.S. national park. The Haleakala crater, at ten thousand feet above sea level, is about the size of Manhattan. (Technically, the valley at the top of the summit is not a crater, because it was formed by slow, steady water erosion over time, not by volcanic activity.) Covered with cinder cones in astounding shades of brown, red, and green—called the "paint pot" of the fire goddess Pele—it looks like a surreal desert or even what you might imagine the surface of Mars might look like. Acoustic experts have declared it the quietest place on Earth, asserting that the crater's sound levels are "near the very threshold of human hearing."

Dad used to take us camping at Haleakala, which I will call "the crater" because that's what it has been called since the early 1800s. We would stay in one of the three cabins, called Hōlua, Kapalaoa, and Palikū, built by the Civilian Conservation Corps in the late 1930s. These cabins were—and still are—rustic, with no electricity or indoor plumbing. The water was outside the cabin, but because it was untreated, it had to be filtered before we could use it.

Haleakala means "House of the Sun," and it offers perhaps the most spectacular sunrises on the planet. People make the very early morning trip up there to be at the summit to witness one of nature's most impressive shows. Today, it takes a couple of hours to make the drive; when I was a kid, it took even longer. Waking up on the summit to see the sun come up was truly an extraordinary experience—one time it even snowed! My folks took us all up to the top of the crater, and I saw snow for the first time. They wanted to take a picture of our family in the snow. I remember having to wait in the car until they were ready to shoot the picture because I didn't have any shoes on! I was wearing only a sweatshirt and jeans. I got out, ran to get in the photo, and then dashed back to the car. I also remember jumping out of the car into a pile of corn snow and trying to make a snow angel. That day was quite an adventure.

My friends and I got our driver licenses when we turned fifteen, so on the weekends the mountain became our playground.

We'd meet up at the Maui Country Club in Spreckelsville, where my mom and dad were members, wait to see who showed up with a car or truck, and hop in. We would go camping and fishing, surfing and swimming. We were young and so full of energy that nothing could tire us.

One of our favorite things to do was what we called riding the flumes. In the pineapple fields in Makawao, the plantation had created a cement track that ran downhill. Water flowed down the track into a pool. You would jump in at the top of the track and ride the track down like a speed course. You would come to a screeching halt right at a barrier wall, which you had to climb over to get out of the flume. You had to lie flat on the way down because the cement was rough, and you could tear your shorts if you tried to go down sitting up. Nevertheless, we inevitably came out with scrapes on our bottoms, bleeding, and with our suits torn. Of course, the company didn't like us doing it.

My friend Kim von Tempsky's dad knew someone who ran the East Maui irrigation company. This land was a part of the island that was highly secure. It provided a water source for the cane fields across much of the island, and they were careful to make sure it stayed clean. But it was an appealing place to explore, and Kim's dad would get permission for us to hike there. We had to pass through as many as ten gates to travel up ten miles. We had some excellent adventures on the trails that ran up into the rain forest on the east side of the island. It would be an all-day adventure of hiking and picnics in what felt like sacred land; generally no one was allowed there.

Of course, going to Hana was a great treat. Today, the Hana Highway is famous for its countless torturous curves and one-lane bridges. Nearly all of its sixty-four miles travel through a tropical microclimate. In the sixties, the road beyond Haiku wasn't paved, which made the drive even more exciting and long enough to require camping overnight. Hana was an isolated town then, far from so-called civilization. I can remember the locals coming out to stand in their yards and wave at us because people were going by. We would stop in The Hasegawa General Store for any supplies we might have left at home. That little store sold everything from packaged food, hardware, and fishing gear to souvenirs and was made famous in 1961 with a song by the same name.

Our destination was Kipahulu, just past Hana. Kipahulu is part of Haleakala National Park now, but you'd only know it by looking at a map. You cannot reach it by road from the summit, and the landscape is a rainforest—utterly distinct from the arid desert of Haleakala—reaching down to a stunning blue ocean of waves battering spectacular black lava cliffs.

But when I was going there with my brothers and our friends, there wasn't a park ranger in sight. We explored the jungle as if it were our private domain.

We camped at what we called the "seven sacred pools," officially known now as the Pools of 'Ohe'o. (Apparently, there are more than seven, and no one can vouch for any ancient Hawaiians considering these pools sacred.) We would night dive for fish. We swam in the underwater caves at Wai'anapanapa. We hiked the Pipiwai Trail, a four-mile roundtrip past streams to the Bamboo Forest and a magnificent waterfall, and to all the pools above the seven sacred pools. We'd have guava fights, squishing the soggy ones on each other's heads, and going for a swim to wash it off afterward. We slept on the beaches, with no one to tell us it wasn't allowed.

Back downcountry, we enjoyed similar adventures in La Perouse Bay and Kanaloa, just past Wailea. In those days, the south side of the island was pretty isolated. The beaches were the best on the island, but it was a desert, and there was virtually no public water supply, so few people lived there. We had friends who owned dive boats, so we would dive all around the island. We would camp overnight and cook the fish we caught for our dinner. We would dive for lobsters (yes, Hawaii has its own species of lobster called *ula*), and sometimes we would snag twenty or thirty! We would surf in the morning before heading home. Other days, we'd camp and surf at Ma'alaea, or we would head up to Honolua Bay and Lahaina Harbor.

It was early morning when Jimbo and I loaded our scuba gear into Dave Padgett's dive boat in Ma'alaea. With our spearguns, we headed to Kaho'olawe, the smallest of the Hawaiian islands. Starting in World War II, the U.S. Navy used the island, just six miles from Maui, for a bombing range. (Luckily, it's uninhabited, because it's still littered with grenades, bombs, and other projectiles. We were allowed to dive there in the seventies—now access is restricted.)

I sat on the edge of the boat in my scuba gear, holding my six-foot-long, three-pronged aluminum spear. When we reached the east cliffs of the deserted island, I rolled backward off the boat into the water, toward a beautiful array of coral along a cliff line that dropped off into a bottomless, deep-blue abyss.

Jimbo and Dave led the way. We descended sixty feet, looking for whatever came our way. I remember looking over my shoulder to see that nothing was coming on my blind side, as the depth was somewhat unnerving. Seeing a small papio along the cliff face, I cocked the surgical rubber and took my shot. My spear hit his tail fin. I would have to lead my aim ahead of the moving fish to make a good shot.

Frustrated, I turned to swim forward. I saw Dave chasing three large *ulua*, also known as giant trevally, into a large cave while Jim hung outside. At that moment, I noticed three more ulua come around the submerged point, heading to the cave. I swam toward the opening, hoping to meet them.

Suddenly, they saw Jimbo and turned away. A huge one came right toward me! I guess it didn't see me until it was about five feet away. It turned, exposing its side. This time I was ready with my three-prong cocked. I aimed for its head and released the spear. Bullseye!

As it quivered at the end of the spear, I started hyperventilating. The fish was the largest I had ever seen underwater. The fish shuddered and slowly sank to the bottom, where I pinned him against the coral.

I looked toward the cave to see another enormous ulua coming out at full speed, streaming from a wound that David had inflicted. It could have been swimming the speed of a motorboat—I've never seen a fish swim so fast. I watched in awe as he swam into the depths and out of sight in seconds.

That fish was long gone by the time Dave emerged from the cave. He helped me swim my ulua back to the boat. He jumped up into the boat and helped me lift the massive fish.

"This isn't my fish!" he said.

"No, it's not," I said. "Your fish swam out into the deep blue and escaped. But thanks for the help!"

That fish weighed an astounding eighty-nine pounds. It was a luckier shot than I realized once my dad applied his surgical mastery on the cutting board. My spear had not fully penetrated the fish but had severed the spinal cord, allowing me to land my prey.

We froze dozens of fillets and ate well for the rest of the summer.

On another Kaho'olawe dive experience, Jimbo and I were free diving along the north side of the island in about forty feet of water. It was a beautiful, balmy morning with glassy water, and the boat was anchored about five hundred feet away from where we were diving for fish. I dove down over a couple of nice papio and took a good shot. I speared one and swam to the surface. The other fish continued to circle below. Since it would take some time to get to the boat, I decided to shove the fish I'd caught down my swim trunks and dive back down after the second fish. I knew this was a dangerous thing to do, but I had no stringer, and I only intended one more dive before returning to the boat with my fish.

I swam deep down to the bottom with the tail of my fish sticking out the front of my shorts and took a few shots at the other fish, which was very nervous to see me and holding its distance. With my air running out, I gave up. I turned and started ascending toward the surface, which took some time to reach. About halfway up, my instinct told me to turn around. I did, only to see a white-tip shark about forty feet away, coming in my direction, and quickly!

I reached into my shorts and pulled on the papio's tail, intending to offer it up for the shark's lunch instead of me. But the fish spines stuck painfully into my palm. *Bad idea*, I thought.

Now the shark was arching with its fins down in a very agitated fashion. It was just ten feet away!

I cocked my spear. Holding it about two feet away from my groin, I thrust the tip three times at it—to about an inch from his nose to let it know I didn't like this. It got my vibe and turned, but apparently not to leave.

The shark opened its eye and looked right into mine. I saw my life pass in front of me. It made another turn and swam about eight feet away. When it turned back to me, I could see intent in its eye. I knew I had to offer up my papio sacrifice, and quickly.

I ripped open the buttons on my trunks to let the fish out, all the while kicking backward and swimming away from the shark as fast as I ever swam in any contest.

The fish descended below me. The shark made a quick meal of my catch, and I was never so happy to let him have it!

I finally reached the surface, blowing the water out my snorkel and trying to catch my breath after a deep dive with a visitor that I didn't want to see again. It was an uncomfortable swim back to the boat—I was afraid to take my eyes off where I had left the shark. But I made it.

If you take chances, you have to be prepared and aware of the unexpected! I was very, very lucky, indeed!

At home in Kahului, we recognized practically everyone wherever we went, whether it was to the grocery store or the airport. At one time, Kahului looked a lot like Paia and Lahaina do now, with charming old shops running along Kaahumanu and Puunene avenues. They eventually tore the shops down to build the Kahului Shopping Center in 1951, known simply as "the shopping center" on Maui. It had a grocery store, a clothing store, a drug store, a barbershop, a restaurant, and even a photo studio and a jewelry store. Retired folks would hang out under the monkeypod trees to "talk story," as we say in Hawaii.

Dad would have breakfast at Toda Drugs in the shopping center and hold court with all the locals. They laughed a lot, talking story, and sharing jokes and fishing tales.

Dad arranged for us to have our first jobs at Toda Drugs. I went with my brothers, and we'd sweep the sidewalk on Saturday mornings. They paid us a quarter each, and they'd feed us a stack of pancakes. So those were good mornings.

When I got old enough for a proper summer job, Dad introduced me to Mr. Burnett at the chicken farm. We didn't have a lot of opportunity for jobs, and most of them were in agriculture. My older brothers, Guy and Jim, worked for Mr. Burnett shoveling chicken manure from under the pens. Dad called them "pilots." When I asked him what that meant, Guy spoke up and said, "It means I 'pile it' here, and I 'pile it' there."

On Fridays, they slaughtered the chickens. Guy and Jim helped with that, too. In addition to their meager pay, they each took home one chicken and a carton of eggs.

My interview with Mr. Burnett didn't go so well. When he asked me why I had come to see him, I said, "Well, Dad says that I should come over here and work, but I'm not sure I want to. I just don't think I'm ready to do this kind of work."

I didn't get the job. I don't remember being too disappointed.

Somehow, I managed to miss out on working in the pineapple fields, too. After my brothers worked at the chicken farm, they worked at Maui Land & Pineapple. They would get up at four-thirty to drive up to the plantation in Hali'imaile by six in the morning. They were paid around a dollar an hour, and maybe twenty cents more if they worked overtime. To guard themselves from the sharp points of the pineapple leaves and the sun, they wore boots and leather chaps over their jeans, goggles, gloves, and a hat. Remember, this was summer in Hawaii, and it was hot. Those sharp leaves tangled up among all the pineapples, making it hard to walk the planting lines. The first person to walk along the rows "breaks the line." It's not an easy walk.

Guy and Jim got the worst jobs, of course, because they were the summer help. They did spot planting, crawling along the ground to fill in empty spots where pineapples were missing or had died. They did a lot of other lousy jobs, too. Anne worked in a pineapple cannery, which was easier, but still didn't sound like a lot of fun. After hearing them talk at the dinner table, I knew I had no interest in working in the fields.

I had no better incentive to get a good education.

Through the eighth grade, I went to Kaunoa, a little school about five miles from home, in Spreckelsville. Spreckelsville was a company town that, at one time, had the largest sugar plantation in the world. Kaunoa was an "English-standard" school. These schools were established in Hawaii in the 1920s—thirty years before Hawaii would become a state—to emphasize English fluency. In those early days, most of the students attending English-standard schools were whites.

But Kaunoa was not a segregated school. It was considered the haole school, but it was racially diverse. They merged Spreckelsville School—the camp school—with Kaunoa when I was in fourth or fifth grade. Those students were mostly Japanese and Chinese, and of course, their parents wanted them to have as good an education as the haole kids.

I had plenty of friends who weren't haole. My folks raised me to treat everyone with respect and kindness. While those kids were perfecting their English, we haole kids were learning pidgin. Hawaiian Pidgin English is a Hawaiian dialect—slang, really—originating in the camps and spoken by a majority of residents. The language is simple but speaking it "properly" is not. The nuances are a little tricky. It helps to be immersed in it from youth, which we experienced when the camp kids showed up at Kaunoa. We all became bilingual, essentially, ironically preserving the dialect.

After school, Mom would pick us up and drive us back to the Puunene Sugar Mill, and we would go to swim team workouts at the pool HC&S built next to the mill. Our coach, Benny Castor, learned to swim in the irrigation ditches on Maui. It was pretty much the only afterschool activity available to us. Mom's intention, I'm sure, wasn't so much to see us develop into great swimmers, but to wear us out so we'd come home exhausted and ready for bed soon after dinner.

In the fourth grade, I participated in a grade school meet amongst the schools on Maui. Because of all my ocean experience, I came to the meet a strong swimmer. I won second place in the fifty-yard backstroke after only two weeks of training. The backstroke would prove to be my event, but not for several years. When I was thirteen, I packed up all my clothes—mostly hand-me-downs from my brothers—and followed Guy and Jim to Hawaii Prep Academy, a boarding school on the Big Island. I don't remember much about school, but I'll never forget getting up at four-thirty in the morning to swim in an ocean pool made of rafts cobbled together with sixty-gallon drums and telephone poles and swarming with all sorts of sucking and biting sea creatures. Little did I guess how that backwater training commitment would lead to a record-setting swimming career and a lifetime camaraderie with Olympic champions.

Swimming with Sea Urchins

"Fred!" a voice whispered. "Fred! Wake up!"

I felt someone nudge my shoulder, and I pulled myself out of a dream in which I had been swimming with sharks and jellyfish. It was more of a nightmare, and one that happened daily since I started working out in the ocean instead of the high school swimming pool.

My roommate, Tom Cannon, grumbled in his sleep and rolled over. I envied him. It was four-thirty in the morning, and my math teacher and coach, Gerry Damon, had somehow managed to talk me into an extra workout three days a week. It had sounded like a good idea when, one afternoon after swim practice, he offered to sneak me out of the dorm early in the morning and drive me to the pool in a car he borrowed from a school administrator. We had to be quiet about it because a school policy insisted that students get a full eight hours of sleep each night, and this early wakeup call came after I'd slept maybe six. But Coach Damon had seen some talent in me, and he asked if I wanted to take on more workouts. I agreed—flattered, excited, and eager to validate his expectations.

I was a sophomore at Hawaii Prep Academy on the Big Island, and I had been on the school swim team for two years. Education came first for the Haywood boys, so the fact that our snazzy private school didn't have a swimming pool didn't matter too much to my brothers and me. Guy, Jim, and I were used to traveling to swim practice, so riding for nearly an hour on a bus each afternoon to swim in the pool at Honoka'a High School was no trouble. Swimming was second nature to us and second in priority to our schoolwork. We were our father's sons, after all.

I quickly got my bearings as I peeked at Coach Damon, who was shining a flashlight in my face, and I jumped out of bed to pull on my swimsuit and grab my sweater. Mornings at the ocean are always cold, even in Hawaii.

When Coach Damon pulled up to the harbor, it was still pitch black. The sun wouldn't come up for another hour. He parked the car facing the harbor and left it running with the lights shining on the pool. If you could call it a pool.

Coach Damon had fashioned a six-lane frame in the ocean of plywood, with sixty-gallon drums floating rafts on either end, connected by telephone poles running the twenty-five-yard length. He moored it in a corner of Kawaihae Harbor, which was only a fifteen-minute drive from school, making my early morning swim possible. Well, it served as a fine pool for me as long as I didn't think about the sharks and jellyfish that sometimes considered the pool theirs that early in the morning. Back then, we didn't have swim goggles, so I got "surfer's eye," or *pterygium*, from swimming in the ocean. Pterygium is a scar on the white of the eye, which I had to have surgically removed.

Swimming in the ocean requires a certain grit that most swimmers never have to acquire. One day, when I drifted on my kickboard too close to the pilings that held up the pier, I felt a sudden sharp pain in my thigh. I practically flew out of the water. I looked down to see a dozen six-inch-long sea urchin spines lodged in my leg.

Often at practice we would swim down the coast from one beach to another—a good mile and a half. The coach would start everyone on a clock based on how fast they swam. He always put me last because I was the fastest. Training in the ocean gave me an extraordinary edge that would position me for a national championship a couple of years later.

But at that time, I was focused only on my predawn swim. I slithered into the ocean to light the lantern on the raft. For the next hour and a half, I swam backstroke down one length of the twenty-five-yard pool, and I swam back practicing my freestyle stroke with Coach Damon timing me from the shore. As the sky brightened, we called it quits for the day, and he drove me back to school for my well-earned breakfast. I continued this double workout three days a week for what was our relatively short three-month swimming season. I thought I was putting in a tremendous effort! I had no idea how much more I would be challenged in just a year.

Meeting Mark Spitz

n the summer of 1965, between my sophomore and junior years, I flew to California with my brother Bill and a dozen other swimmers from Hawaii for a coast-to-coast swimming exhibition. The renowned Hawaii swim coach Soichi Sakamoto loaded us up in a Greyhound bus—our tickets cost fifty dollars for fifty days! He took us to schools and meets across the country, from San Francisco to New York and back to Los Angeles. This tour was my first experience of the mainland, my first opportunity to swim against some of the best athletes in the country, and my first introduction to a world-class coach.

Soichi Sakamoto was justifiably considered the best swimming coach in the world in the 1940s. In the late thirties, he started coaching Maui plantation children who were swimming in the irrigation ditches that watered the sugar cane on an HC&S plantation. These kids had nowhere to cool off in the hot Maui summers. As many as a hundred splashed in the ditches until they were run off by the plantation foremen. Sakamoto, an elementary school teacher and Boy Scout leader, persuaded plantation authorities to let him supervise the children and teach them formal swimming skills. Never mind that he had no formal swimming skills—he couldn't even swim himself! But he did know how to build character and instill athletic discipline in kids.

Those plantation irrigation ditches were eight feet wide and four feet deep, similar to a swimming lane in a pool, but with a current bringing water to the fields. Sakamoto trained his athletes to swim against the current of the irrigation water. The powerful exertion required to swim "upstream" presented a natural resistance, increased the swimmers' strength, and developed in them a more efficient stroke. When the swimmers drifted back down with the current, they were able to practice form. The combination pioneered interval training in which the swimmers alternated high-intensity upstream sprint sessions with a relaxed downstream recovery.

"In that ditch, the current coming down offered them natural resistance," Sakamoto told the *Honolulu Advertiser* in 1984. "And when they swam up, they were developing a stroke that was very efficient and practical. If they had done it in entirely still water, I don't think it would have developed. Drifting down in the current gave them very relaxed movement, gave them a very beautiful style. Gradually, everything started to fall into place."

HC&S eventually helped build those kids a proper swimming pool in Puunene, and Sakamoto coached his swimmers to win meets all over Hawaii. It didn't take long for the University of Hawaii to recruit Sakamoto to a campus on the Big Island, which is how he found me and invited me to participate in swim meets across the country.

Sakamoto pulled countless children out of the rough irrigation ditches and into swimming pools, teaching them more than a few swim strokes. No one knows how many Olympic swimmers he inspired. But what thrilled Sakamoto was in changing kids' lives. He got us to think bigger, to place an importance on giving back, and to value the benefit of hard work. I was proud and delighted when, at a mainland hotel pool, he asked me to swim across the pool so my teammates could see my stroke. Swimming for him that summer influenced my outlook on life—and literally changed it.

The first stop on our nationwide tour was Foothill College, just half an hour from the San Francisco airport. Here we were to compete in a swim meet with kids from around the San Francisco area. I was mesmerized by the enormity of my surroundings—the magnificent natatorium, the number and talent of the kids participating in the meet, the heightened activity of life on the mainland, the sheer noise that filled the air when a hundred or more kids are having fun in a pool.

As I sat on the side of the pool with my brother and my teammates, waiting for my turn to swim, I felt a tap on my shoulder. I turned around to see a good-looking boy my age standing behind me, looking at me curiously. He was skinny but muscled, with dark hair and deep-set dark eyes. He wore a Speedo swimsuit, as we all did, and his hands grasped the towel hanging around his neck.

I stood up to face him and smiled.

"Hi," I said.

"Are you from Hawaii?" he asked.

"Yes," I replied. "Yes, I am. My name's Fred. Fred Haywood. Who are you?"

"I'm Mark. Mark Spitz," he replied. "I used to live in Hawaii. I always wanted to meet someone from Hawaii."

A dozen of us from Hawaii were sitting on the side of the pool that day. A kid named Mark Spitz wanted to meet someone from Hawaii, and he tapped on my shoulder. Was it synchronicity? Who knows why he wanted to meet me?

Of course, that day, I had no idea that Mark Spitz would go on to be one of the world's great swimmers. I only knew that to watch him in the pool was an inspiration. He was a magnificent athlete, and he won every event he swam.

Mark moved with his family to Honolulu when he was two years old. Like me, he learned to swim in the ocean, swimming at Waikiki Beach every day. Four years later, the Spitz family moved back to California, where Mark joined a local swim club. His talent was evident by the time he turned fourteen, and his family moved to Santa Clara, where Mark could swim for George Haines, coach of the Santa Clara Swim Club.

At just fifteen years old, Mark outpaced everyone else's ability—including mine. I was accustomed to placing first in meets in Hawaii. But not on that summer tour. I was way behind the talent I encountered. At best, I might have swum fastest among the slowest swimmers.

That summer day at a college pool in a small town outside San Francisco was the first day of what would prove to be a lifelong friendship. It also was the catalyst for my championship swimming career in which I would train under another world-class coach and swim with some of the finest athletes in the country.

When I returned in the fall to Hawaii Prep for my junior year, I told my coach that I met a guy on the summer swim trip who was really good.

"This kid was incredible!" I told Coach Damon. "He swims at Santa Clara High School in California. His name is Mark Spitz."

"Well, you should go swim with him," Coach Damon said.

"Why would I do that?" I asked. "How can I do that?"

"You could move to California and finish high school at Santa Clara."

Coach Damon was my math teacher, too, and math was my strongest subject. I was astounded that my swim coach would encourage me to go to another school.

"You know," he said, "if you go swim with Spitz, I guarantee you that you will get into a better college than if you stay here and get straight As."

Every haole kid knew his ticket off the plantation was a good college education, and that could only be achieved—at the time—on the mainland. I was attending Hawaii Prep to make sure I could get into a good college. But my grades reflected my expectations of myself, not my ambition. I was barely maintaining a B-minus grade point. After all, my swim training with its double workouts was really taking it out of me (or so I thought at the time). I was tired. I wanted to have more fun. I didn't have the extra time to put into studying. At sixteen, I simply wasn't inspired.

"Well, that sounds good to me," I replied. "Can you help me do that?"

And Coach Damon did.

His encouragement that day led to another life-changing shift for me, one that would set up my success in the water for a decade. I wasn't aware of it at the time—I didn't have a big "aha" moment—but I was experiencing the formation of my life's philosophy. Looking back on it, I can see how my dad taught me an approach that has proven over five decades to guide me to success over five decades, time after time. It wasn't "Follow Your Bliss," or "Life Is What You Make It," or any other kitschy watchword. My evolving philosophy was much more straightforward: just try what's next.

Coach Damon wrote a letter to George Haines, the Santa Clara High School swim coach.

In the sixties, George Haines's high school swimmers held national records in every event. Leading the Santa Clara Swim Club, Haines trained more swimmers inducted into the International Swimming Hall of Fame than any other swim club in the world. He took the team to forty-four national championships and coached twenty-six Olympic swimmers. The 1968 Olympics would prove to be the heyday of the Santa Clara Swim Club team.

To be able to swim for Haines in my last year in high school would be a true testament to my potential and a harbinger for my future. Haines wrote back after a couple of weeks and said he would welcome me to his team. I was invited to swim with athletes who would, in the coming years, bring home an incredible amount of gold.

My coach then called my parents—a big deal in those days when long-distance calls cost money. He suggested that the opportunity offered me a chance to advance my swimming and improve my scholastics.

Dad asked Coach Damon to put me on the phone.

"Is this what you want to do?" Dad asked me.

"Yes, Dad," I told him. "I think it will give me an opportunity to improve in swimming and help me get into a better college."

My parents agreed to send me to California for my senior year. I was going to California for an education. I enjoyed swimming, and I was good at it, but I was not passionate about it. I knew quality higher education was essential if I wanted to live on Maui and have a decent future. My B-minus grades would have earned me acceptance to an average college or university, but if I went to a better school, I had a better chance to excel later in life. Moving to California was a good opportunity, and it just might be my vehicle to a better future. What did I imagine that future to hold? I had no idea. I was only sixteen. All I knew was that this chance to swim—and, more importantly, go to school—in Santa Clara was my ticket out of a life of drudgery working in the pineapple or sugar fields.

Senior Year in Santa Clara

The Santa Clara swimming community was close, and all the families were very involved. Looking back, I expect Coach George Haines greatly influenced that. Haines took the time to get to know each of his swimmers, guiding fifty-three of them to Olympic championships—including Don Schollander, Donna deVarona, and, of course, Mark Spitz.

I wasn't the only kid who left home to swim at Santa Clara with George. (We called him George.) He trained as many as three hundred swimmers at a time, and if my experience was typical, he made an effort to get to know each of us personally and make us feel significant. George knew how to motivate us, and he made training fun, which I liked, of course. He also had a solid code of ethics, which I appreciated because it reminded me of my dad. He was like a father figure to me, and I fell quickly into the welcoming community at Santa Clara.

I moved to Santa Clara as soon as I finished my junior year at Hawaii Prep in May. The team practiced all summer, and I wanted to get right to work. I lived with the Finneran family during the summer. Sharon Finneran had won a silver medal at the 1964 Summer Olympics in Tokyo just a year before. Her brother, Mike, was a diver, and he went to the Olympics in 1972.

When school started, I moved in with the Diaz family. Harry, Lisa, and Marcella were the kids in this Mexican-Irish family. I just loved the Mexican food Mrs. Diaz prepared. My parents paid them room and board. At that point, Harry Diaz and Mark Spitz were my only friends. We would hang out together and carpool to workouts.

We swam six days a week, from eight to ten o'clock in the morning, and went back to the pool every afternoon at four to swim till dinnertime. We were swimming as many as six miles a day in short burst intervals. The pool had clocks at each corner, so I could see what my times were whenever I made a turn at either end of the pool. I was a long way from that ocean pool and getting stung by jellyfish.

Because my swim season at Hawaii Prep was only three months in the winter, when I arrived in Santa Clara, it had been almost six months since I had trained. I was out of shape—and way behind my teammates in the skills department. I hadn't started swimming full time until those double workouts at Hawaii Prep. I was sixteen years old then. These boys had been swimming seriously since they were very young. I had a lot of catching up to do.

I had a sense of the possibility—it was becoming my nature to look for the bright side. My dad had taught me to face any confrontation by stepping out of judgment and into curiosity. What might I learn or discover if I set aside my idea of how something should be? Doing so was never easy. It took practice to stop and wonder, and sometimes it took courage. I swallowed my pride, remembering the day my dad shoved me off the boat and into the water, and I prepared once again to sink or swim.

Those workouts were eye-opening—and grueling. George had finessed his ability to train a large number of swimmers in the eight-lane, fifty-meter pool in summers. (Our high school practice pool was twenty-five yards long.) He would line us up, five in a lane on each end, and start us five seconds apart. The fastest swimmers would go first, then the next fastest, and so on. The fastest guys were swimming side by side. If a kid behind you swam faster, he would tap on your feet to pass.

I was number one in Hawaii in freestyle, so I assumed that's what I would swim at Santa Clara. That put me swimming a distant second to Mark, whose best stroke was freestyle, followed by the butterfly. But my freestyle didn't go anywhere, and I wasn't improving much.

The whole summer was exhausting. My pace was flat. I wasn't swimming any faster than when I left Hawaii. *Wow, this is so hard*, I would think.

I was really in the doldrums. It never occurred to me to keep in mind that this was my first chance to experience the challenge of world-class professional training. I was swimming with the some of the best high school swimmers in the country: Mark Spitz, Mitch Ivey, Bob Jameson, Rick Eagleston, and Jack Faunce. Little did I know the strain I was putting on my heart.

George frequently had us swimming sets of one-hundred-yard lengths on the minute-fifteen—meaning that we would swim a hundred yards and start again a minute and fifteen seconds after the start whistle. We would repeat that hundred yards ten times. After each set of ten, we'd get a five-minute break.

George had discovered what Doc Counsilman and maybe a handful of top swim coaches knew—the power of interval training. Instead of just swimming lengths at a steady pace until we reached, say, a mile, we would swim a hundred yards at a time at high speed and take short rests of maybe fifteen seconds. We did intervals with fifty-, one-hundred-, two-hundred-, and four-hundred-yard swims. Today this is a common practice called high-intensity interval training. In the mid-1960s, though, this innovative performance-enhancing routine made a huge difference. George's swimmers were crushing world records.

When we finished a set, we would check our pulse for fifteen seconds and multiply that number by four to get our beats-per-minute rate. We were shooting to get above two hundred. Then, we'd take it again after a minute or two to see how fast our heart rates would come down. The resting pulse was more important—the lower, the better. Mine was around forty-eight or forty-nine beats per minute. Mark's resting pulse rate was forty-two.

No matter how hard I pushed it in the freestyle, Mark would always beat me by two body lengths or more every single time. I was repeating a hundred-yard freestyle in fifty-five or fifty-eight seconds, which would give me, at most, twenty seconds to rest before pounding it again.

On one particular day, I was swimming the backstroke with Mitch Ivey, cruising at about a minute-four to a minute-five. That left me with only ten seconds of rest before I had to go again. Mitch was leaving me in his wake, too, finishing in just under a minute. At the end of the ten sets, I got out of the pool and asked the coach if I could take a break. I felt exhausted, more so than usual. My head was spinning. My heart was pounding. I felt like I was going to faint. I somehow made it to the locker room and sat under the shower, wondering what was making me feel so bad. Ten minutes later, I felt recovered, and I jumped back into the pool. I didn't realize I had just experienced my first atrial flutter. It wouldn't be the last, but it would be years before I realized what was happening to me. I've since had repeated experiences and subsequent medical treatment for atrial fibrillation. I learned recently that many of my swimming colleagues have suffered similar heart conditions, causing me to question the impact of high-intensity interval training on the long-term health of high-performance athletes.

The Santa Clara Swim Club and its Olympic-caliber athletes had attracted the attention of John du Pont, and he trained with the team in the early sixties. The eccentric heir to the DuPont fortune had dropped out of college after a year and was indulging his athletic passions. By the time I arrived, he was no longer swimming, but he came with a video camera—this was 1966, mind you, decades before they were even remotely affordable. He taped us swimming underwater through a window in the side of the pool. He had a one-inch reel-to-reel Ampex video recorder. For the first time, we all got to see ourselves swim. Sure, we had still photos of ourselves in the water and coming off the blocks, but I had never seen myself in motion. It helped me to improve my stroke when I could see the position of my arm underwater.

But nothing improved my stroke like the advice of my teammate Mitch Ivey.

Five Minutes to Fast

Mitch had been swimming at Santa Clara for several years before I got there. He had grown up next door to George Haines. He was number one in the nation in high school backstroke, which was my second-best stroke after the freestyle.

So here I was, competing in the Santa Clara Swim Club pool with Mitch Ivey in backstroke and Mark, who was number one in freestyle. While I was stoked by the challenge of swimming against Mark, it was pretty clear to me if I wanted to win anything at Santa Clara, it wasn't going to happen in the freestyle.

One day—one that would prove to be the most important day of my swimming career—we were swimming our usual forty repeats of a hundred yards. The first twenty, I swam freestyle with Mark in the lane next to me, and as usual, he was ahead of me by one or two body lengths on each repeat. I could tell how well I was doing by the size of the bubbles from his kick.

When I was swimming freestyle in the pool, I could look across to Mark in the other lane. I might not see him if he was ahead, but I could see the size of the bubbles he was kicking up. The smaller the bubbles, the further behind I was, and his bubbles tended to be pretty small.

After twenty repeats in the lane next to Mark, I decided I'd turn over and swim backstroke with Mitch, who was swimming in the other lane next to me. When I was swimming backstroke, I didn't look for bubbles, but I could see his arms in the air. You can easily view everyone in the pool if you are leading a backstroke race.

It was ugly in the beginning. In the first ten sets of a hundred yards, I lost to Mitch every single time. My times for a hundred yards averaged a minute and three seconds, up to a minute six. Mitch was averaging a minute, crushing me by five seconds or more. The beating hurt more because my rest time was whittled down to ten seconds or less, while Mitch could take a breather for more than fifteen seconds.

After ten of these trounces, we stopped for our five-minute break. I was gasping for breath and holding the lane line. Mitch looked over at me. I knew I wasn't a pretty sight. He concurred.

"Wow, Fred, your backstroke is really ugly," he said. "You're bobbing and weaving and hitting the lane lines. It just looks horrible."

I was blown away that he could be so insulting. My experience of everyone at Santa Clara had been welcoming, even friendly. I clenched my jaw and tightened my fist underwater where he couldn't see it. I was about two feet away from him. I so wanted just to swing at him, but I wasn't going to do that. Dad had taught me better.

It took everything I had to set aside my judgment and be curious about how I might react to Mitch. I took a couple of breaths. I paused.

"Well, Mitch," I said, "you have the prettiest stroke I've ever seen in my life. What do I have to do to look like you?"

He took the bait.

"Oh. Well, get out of the pool, and I'll show you something."

I hopped up onto the pool deck. Mitch picked up a small towel, wadded it up like a ball, and handed it to me.

"Hold it over your head like you're going to swim backstroke," he told me. "Now throw it at the pool deck. You want it to land next to your baby toe."

I did. It landed six feet from my foot. At least Mitch didn't laugh at me. I had to give him credit for that.

"You've got to tuck your elbow behind your back and come right in next to your hip. That will make the towel land near your baby toe."

I tossed the towel right back in the spot it had landed the first time. I tried it again. I was getting pretty frustrated. But Mitch didn't laugh or give up on me. He was proving to be a pretty good coach. In fact, in less than ten years, after three national championships and medaling in the 1968 and 1972 Olympics, Mitch Ivey would assume George Haines's job as coach of the Santa Clara Swim Club.

"Okay, here's what you've got to do. You need to rotate your shoulders. Lift your shoulder up in the air over your nose." He tapped my right arm, the one holding the towel, and pulled it forward over my nose. "Slide the left one way behind you, and drop your elbow behind your back."

He pushed my left shoulder back, and I twisted my torso so that my right shoulder was over my nose, and my left shoulder moved back behind my hip.

Wow! I always thought I had to swim with a straight arm and stay flat on my back in the water. I didn't know I should rotate my body to swim backstroke.

This time I fired the towel down with my right arm—now positioned in the way Mitch instructed. And I got it! It landed on the pool deck right next to my right toe. I tossed it a couple more times, hitting my target each time. I passed the towel to my left hand and tossed it, twisting my torso in the opposite direction, and I got it. It landed by my left baby toe!

After a few more tosses from each arm, placing that towel right by my feet, I heard the whistle. Our five-minute break was up. I was grinning from my discovery. I patted Mitch on the back and thanked him. I was grateful for the lesson. More than that, I was eager to try my new stroke. We jumped back in the pool, taking the two center lanes for our last set of ten-by-one-hundred-yard swims.

I beat Mitch in the first hundred yards, swimming it in fifty-nine seconds!

We went again. I beat him again, maybe by half a body length. I had increased my speed by at least five seconds. For the first time, I experienced the full fifteen seconds of rest before the next hundred yards. I beat him again. And again. Then again, until the last repeat.

Mitch looked at me like he wondered who I was—or what he had just done.

"Okay," he said before the tenth repeat. "Let's race."

That's when the competition heated up. I swam a 56.8 on the fortieth one. That just may have the most important day of my life. That day, in one five-minute coaching session courtesy of my teammate, I cut eight-tenths of a second off my hundred-yard best in the backstroke on my fortieth repeat with a push start.

We were only two of maybe twenty high school swimmers in the pool that day, but Coach George Haines hadn't missed what was going on between Mitch and me.

"Fred, I'm going put you in a dual meet with Mitch this weekend," he said. A dual meet was a competition between just two high schools. "But first, I want to see what you're going to do on your own in the hundred."

The next day, I swam the unofficial one hundred, finishing as fast as I could. George squatted down on the pool deck at the end of the lane with his stopwatch in his hand and the cord dangling between his fingers. I touched the wall and looked up at him.

I knew I had done pretty well. I had no idea how well. George raised his hand, letting the stopwatch slide down along the cord. It dropped right in front of my face, and the little clock spun before me. I reached up to stop the spinning watch. It read "54." Fifty-four seconds flat.

The national high school record at the time was 54.1.

I had just set a new national high school record. Unfortunately, with only Harry Diaz swimming with me in the pool, it was unofficial.

That weekend, as George had promised, I swam against Mitch in a dual meet. Once again, I swam the hundred in fifty-four seconds flat, and that made it official. I broke the national high school record. And I beat Mitch, the national champion, again.

George pulled me aside.

"Hey, look, Fred," he said. "I have to take you to the Nationals."

"What's that?" I asked. "What are Nationals?"

I was genuinely clueless. Except for that bus tour across the country with Sakamoto, I had no idea of the hierarchy of swimming challenges.

"The Nationals are in Dallas," George said, explaining briefly what the National AAU Championship was. He noted that I'd be racing against the best swimmers in the country. "It's in two weeks. This is very exciting. I was only going to take Spitz. But if

I take you, I have to take Mitch, too. His mom would never have it if I left him behind!"

Wow! I thought. *It was worth coming to Santa Clara to swim. I think I'll get into a good college now for sure.*

I was pretty pleased with myself, of course. But I didn't overlook the gratitude I felt for all the folks who helped me get to California—Coach Damon, Coach Sakamoto, and, most especially, my dad. My dad's influence stayed with me even though I was an ocean away from home.

Only One Person in the Pool

The following weekend, before the Nationals in Dallas, I was invited to the Spitz home for dinner for the first time. I was pretty excited. Mark and I were friends, but I still appreciated the chance to hang out with a guy who was such an incredible swimmer. He would become one of the greatest swimmers of all time, holding that honor until 2016 when Michael Phelps collected twenty-eight gold medals—fifty years later! I believed that if you want to fly high, you hang out with eagles, and Mark was a true eagle. I was honored to be able to hang out with him in his nest.

Mark's dad was very different from mine. Instead of teaching his kids humility, as my dad did, Arnold Spitz taught them not just to win, but to want to win.

Mark started swimming when he was eight—much younger than I had been. Two years later, he was swimming an hour and a half every day. Mark was consistently beating older swimmers. He set his first U.S. record when he was ten years old.

His dad was the power force behind his wins.

"Mark?" Mr. Spitz would ask. "How many lanes in a pool?"

"Six," Mark would reply.

"And how many lanes win?"

"One, only one."

In 1964, Mark began swimming with George at Santa Clara. Workouts started at six-thirty in the morning, and his mom drove him forty miles from their home in Walnut Creek before they moved to Santa Clara. The whole family invested in Mark's swimming success. His dad said as much a few years later in an interview with *Sports Illustrated*:

"The greatest motivating factor in Mark's life has been Lenore and myself. Because of what I've given of myself, this is what I created. ... You think this just happens? I've got my life tied up in this kid. There is nothing wrong with parents giving to their children. If people don't like it, the hell with 'em. ... There was a point when I pushed him, I guess, but if I hadn't pushed my son, he would never have been at Santa Clara. ... Swimming isn't everything; winning is. Who plays to lose? I'm not out to lose. I never said to him, 'You're second; that's great.' I told him I didn't care about winning age groups; I care for world records."

And that was precisely my experience with Arnold Spitz.

At dinner that night with Mark, his parents, and his sisters, Heidi and Nancy, the talk turned to the upcoming Nationals. Mark could only enter three events, and his dad was analyzing them to decide of the six Mark could swim, which ones he would be sure to win. I found the conversation exciting—my dad had never taken such a keen interest in whether or not I won anything.

Mr. Spitz was strategizing. He wanted Mark to swim two short races one day and a long one the next. I started to daydream a bit, basking in my luck to be eating dinner with this family. I thought about my friends back on Maui, wondering what they were doing on their Saturday night and what they would think about me if they knew where I was.

Whoa, I thought. *This is everything I dreamed of, right here. To be sitting here with Mark Spitz talking about swimming races.*

I had nothing to say. I was like a little bug on the table, listening.

All of a sudden, Mr. Spitz leaned across the table and asked me, "Well, Fred, what are you swimming? And how are you going to do?"

"Well, Mr. Spitz," I said politely—my dad taught me to be unassuming, "I'm swimming the hundred back. It's the only thing I qualified for. I figure if I can maybe swim a half a second faster, maybe I can get a third place."

Even this was hard for me to say. I realized I was questioning myself, just by claiming that I might win a medal at all. I was brought up in Hawaii to have respect for my elders and always show humility. If I started bragging about something at my parents' dinner table, my siblings would mock me, and my dad would call me to task. (Mom wouldn't say a word—she never uttered a word that wasn't nice and supportive.) Dad would always bring us back to neutral if we got a little big for our britches. If ever there was any self-aggrandizing going on, he would ask, "Well, what makes you feel that way?"

That was Dad.

And while we may have talked about what we wanted to do, we never predicted what we were going to do—we never bragged about a possible accomplishment. So in the Spitz kitchen that night, I was embarrassed to say I hoped to swim half a second faster because I had never done it.

"What do you mean, half a second faster?" Mr. Spitz asked. He wasn't yelling or using any swear words, but he sure sounded like he wanted to. "What does that mean?"

"Well," I replied, "my best time was fifty-four flat last week. Last year, it was 57.4. So if I can go half a second faster, maybe I can get a third place."

Mr. Spitz stared at me. "I just don't understand what you are saying."

I had a feeling he was somehow setting me up, but I couldn't see what might be coming.

"I looked at the NCAA times," I said. "Number six in the backstroke was 53.9. Number one swam a fifty-three flat. If I can go at 53.5, I might be able to win a third place."

When Mr. Spitz asked me the same question for a third time, I answered the same, but pushed my time a tenth of a second better, to 53.4.

He just looked at me. The room was hushed. Maybe a second or two passed between us, but it seemed like time stood still. I could sense that the rest of the Spitz family anticipated with just a bit of awe precisely what was coming.

Mr. Spitz pointed his index finger at me.

"Fred," he said quietly and slowly, never raising his voice but speaking with all the force in the world. "There is only one person in the pool that everyone is going to remember." Then he slammed his fist on the table. The silverware jumped. The plates chattered. "SECOND THROUGH SIXTH ARE ALL LOSERS, AND DON'T YOU EVER FORGET IT!"

I was stunned speechless.

Wow… what was that? I thought. *I'm getting yelled at by Mark's dad because I said I wanted to swim half a second faster, and now I'm a loser!*

We hadn't grown up thinking like that. Nobody was a loser. Dad taught us that participating was just fine, as long as we tried our best. When our best wasn't good enough, we could move on to what was next for us.

I remember walking around in a fog for a couple of days after that dinner at the Spitzes.

What am I going to do? I wondered.

There's only one person everyone is going to remember. Second through sixth are all losers.

I wasn't upset. I wasn't mad at Mr. Spitz for speaking to me like that. When I thought about what my dad might say, I knew what to do. In the same way I calmed my response to Mitch Ivey telling me how ugly my stroke was, I decided to react to Mr. Spitz with curiosity instead of judgment.

That curiosity resulted in this awareness: Mr. Spitz's outburst jolted me into a new way of thinking about winning. That awareness meshed nicely with what I already knew to be true. Even at seventeen, I knew to instill in my belief system what I wanted. I don't know if I got that from swimming or my dad. I just knew I had to believe in what I wanted—and in myself—to be able to achieve it.

A few days before we left for Dallas, I woke up dreaming I won the hundred backstroke. I'd never had swimming dreams. I never swam in the Nationals before, but I dreamt that I'd won it.

This had me curious.

Less than a week later, I got the chance to change my stroke *and* change the way I looked at winning. Can you imagine? Both had an incredible influence on me. It was a dramatic one-two—dramatic having Mitch show me that stroke and beating him, and dramatic sitting at the dinner table and listening to Mr. Spitz.

Then I dreamt that I won that race.

Fred Who?

n April, we headed to Southern Methodist University in Dallas for the Men's National AAU Indoor Swimming Championships. The opportunity astounded me. Even after I arrived in Dallas, I marveled at my fortune. I had been previously ranked fifty-fifth or sixtieth in backstroke in the country. You had to swim it in around fifty-five seconds to qualify. Before Mitch showed me the new stroke, I was several seconds slower. I arrived in Dallas to find I was ranked ninth. I was stoked!

First, we had to qualify. There were eight qualifying heats. Mitch swam in the third or fourth heat, and I watched his race intently, as you can imagine. He swam a 54.7, which meant he wasn't going to make the finals!

"Oh, shit," I said to myself. "He just repeated his best time."

I swam in the last heat, in the lane next to Charlie Hickcox. Charlie, who was in college, had never lost a race.

He had set eight world records between 1967 and 1968. He was named World Swimmer of the Year in 1968. He would go on to win seven NCAA individual titles, nine AAU titles, and two golds at the Pan-American Games.

I was freaking out. Just two weeks earlier, I hadn't even heard of the Nationals. Now I was swimming next to a guy who had never lost a race.

I stood on the edge of the pool, nearly hyperventilating. I had no idea what to do with my body until the race started. So I watched Charlie.

Okay, I said to myself. *I'm just going to copy him.* I shook out my arms and legs, trying to shake away all that nervous energy. Then, when Charlie dove in the pool, turned over, and took a couple of strokes, I dove in, turned over, and took a few strokes. I got out, stretched some more, and breathed.

Finally, it was time. We got up on the starting blocks. We had to put our toes over the edge of the gutter. Then the gun fired, and we were off.

I can remember lots of splashing around me. Everyone was pretty close. All I could do was swim as fast as I could, hoping to pick up that half a second I told Mr. Spitz I wanted.

But I didn't swim half a second faster. I swam 52.9—one whole second faster.

When I touched the wall and looked around, I could see that the crowd was going nuts. A lot of Santa Clara people were there. They had heard about me and knew that this was my first Nationals. Now I had qualified for the finals.

That night, Mark Spitz set the first American record of his career in the one hundred-yard butterfly. And from the middle lane, I swam even faster than my qualifying heat. I won the backstroke at the AAU Indoor Championships with a time of 52.6.

Suddenly, my buddy Brent Burke was about six inches from my face, hollering at me, grabbing me by the shoulders, and jumping up and down, thrilled with the result.

"I can't believe it! YOU DID IT!"

Brent was from Hawaii; we swam against each other in grade school and high school. He knew my history. Brent knew I was a decent swimmer, but he never knew me to be a champion. And here he was, poolside with me at the Nationals, seeing it for himself.

"Shoot, Fred, it's amazing!" Brent continued to shout. "I'm the only one who knows where you were last year!"

I think he was more excited than I was. Of course, I was still stunned from the victory and processing the fact that I had beat Charlie Hickcox.

"You did it!" Brent went on. "I can't believe it. I can't believe it! Fred, it is amazing. You know what I mean?"

I was in a fog. *What the hell's happening here?* I wondered. I wanted to become a decent swimmer in high school to help me get into a good college. I accomplished that two weeks earlier, when I broke the national high school record. Two weeks later, I was the fastest in the nation. I couldn't believe it.

Brent helped me grasp the enormity of my accomplishment.

"You had so much power in that event," he said. "You were so strong. You swam so powerfully in the water. You were just ready to go. And after less than a year swimming at Santa Clara, to become a national champion! It was pretty astounding to watch. Because Hickcox is a big-time swimmer. Yeah. I mean, he is BIG TIME!"

"It was such a huge surprise!" my teammate Rick Eagleston said later, when we were reminiscing about that competition. "We all expected Spitz and a few other guys to win something. I don't think anyone expected you to get to the finals, much less win. But—*whammo!*—it happened, and all of a sudden, you know, you became a star and instantly stepped into the upper echelon of American swimming. It was pretty astonishing."

"Charlie Hickcox had won maybe twenty national championships, and this was going to be the crowning," Jim Gaughran, my coach at Stanford, told me later. "Charlie hadn't lost another race in his entire collegiate career. Well, that was the crowning race because he was a guy who had won three races every year for his entire collegiate career. And you beat him. That was great."

"What's your name?" Charlie asked me after the race, while leaning over our lane divider.

"I'm Fred Haywood," I told him.

"Fred *who?*" he asked.

My teammates in the grandstands heard that, and they started calling me "Fred Who."

Well, the world was about to hear who Fred Haywood was. But first I had to let Dr. Guy Haywood know who just won the AAU Championship in backstroke.

Mark and I got invited up to the press booth. Apparently, we were the first high school swimmers to win at the AAU National Championships.

"The performances by Spitz and Haywood were easily the most significant events on the hot Texas weekend," Kim Chapin wrote in an article titled "The Times Came for Two Teens" for *Sports Illustrated.* "They prompted Indiana's Jim Counsilman to say, 'I don't see how anybody will beat the U.S. in international swimming—ever.'

"Not, at least, as long as there are youngsters like Spitz and Haywood who don't know enough to respect their elders—or the record book."

After the interview, Chapin asked if I wanted to call anyone.

"Yeah," I said. "I'd like to call home." Remember, in those days, long-distance calls cost money. A lot of money, especially to Hawaii.

My dad answered.

"Dad," I hollered into the phone. "I just won the Nationals!"

"What's that? A high school meet?" he asked.

"No, Dad. It's everybody. College and high school. There are a few high schoolers here, but it's mostly college guys. Isn't it great?!"

"Well, what's great about it?"

"Well, everyone's slapping me on the back and telling me how great it was," I said. "So, I thought it was great."

"Well, it's over now, isn't it?" he asked.

"Yeah, it's over."

"Well, I'm really proud of you," he said. "And I'm excited for you. Thanks for calling. I love you."

That was just like my dad. He gave me the kudos I wanted and deserved. But he also wanted to give me a lesson. He tried to bring me back to a humble, neutral place.

"I think it's really unfortunate," my brother Guy told me later, "that our father couldn't help but criticize. His son just got his fifteen seconds of fame—his 'Andy Warhol' moment. He knew what you did—how extraordinary your accomplishment was—and the old man couldn't help but put you in your place."

I wasn't surprised or particularly disappointed. With my dad, if you gloated, you got brought down. It was like I had two fathers, and Dad's approach to parenting was very different from that of Mr. Spitz. My dad, after all, had never even seen me swim.

Teamwork... and a Little Fun

We returned from Dallas to finish out the high school swim season. The Santa Clara High School Swim Club was on fire—unstoppable. At the Central Coast High School Championships after the Nationals, Mark Spitz, Bob Jamison, Rick Eagleston, and I broke another American high school record in the four by one hundred freestyle relay with a time of 3.06.8. Each of us contributed to the win, swimming faster than 47.7, the one hundred-yard freestyle record nationally. Bob led off the relay with a 47 flat, I followed at 47.4. Rick swam a 46.8, and Mark anchored with a 45.6. Spitz touched the wall ahead of the second-place team's flip turn with two lengths left! You can imagine we brought down the house that day.

Next, we had a triangular meet set up with Stanford University and the University of Southern California. Just like a dual meet involves two teams, a triangular meet features three. Stanford and USC had tied the year before in the National Collegiate Athletic Association. That meet was scheduled before we cleaned up at the Nationals. We were pretty stoked about swimming against college guys. But they canceled the meet. Maybe they knew we would have beat them, and they couldn't figure out how to beat us.

Of course, everyone got into really good schools because we were the top of the heap in swimming.

But before we headed off to college, I invited a few of the guys from the swim team to come to Maui. It was a magical time. We rode all over the island—from Honolua Bay to Hana—in a paisley-flowered Jeep.

We took that Jeep home from Hana the back way. You're not supposed to drive the Kaupo Road from Hana because, basically, there is no road. But we felt invincible at the time, so it didn't stop us.

Then we got stuck. But it wasn't a problem—we just all climbed out and lifted the Jeep out of the predicament.

Of course, we couldn't stay out of the water. It was Maui, where there is no place you'd rather be than in the water. Every beach we passed was an excuse to jump out and dive in. We attracted a lot of attention, maybe because the word got around that a bunch of champion swimmers were on the island. Or perhaps it was because we were body surfing, and body surfing isn't all that easy, and folks love to watch it done well. John Ferris broke his nose one day when he ran into Rick Eagleston's head, so my dad, the doctor, fixed him up—he did absolutely nothing to it. He told John his nose wasn't all that far off-center, and it would heal just fine.

I had never been prouder than that summer—returning home a champion, a celebrity of sorts, with my swim team buddies in tow. I will always come home to Maui because Maui will always be home.

From Santa Clara to Stanford

My intention in going to Santa Clara for my senior year in high school was to get into a good university. It worked. The championships spurred a flood of letters to my mailbox offering me scholarships. Remember, I needed a good education if I had any hope of returning to Maui and getting a good job, avoiding a career in the cane fields.

My wins also revealed the love I had for swimming. Until then, swimming was just something I did; I was raised on and in the water. I didn't realize how much I loved to swim until I won some important races. Sure, it's fun to win. But anything is more fun when you're good at it. The perception I had of myself changed. It brought me a sense of importance. It gave me worth. I don't say this to brag. I value humility. I have too much of my father's influence in me, despite the jump-start I got from my "other" dad, Mr. Spitz.

With ten or twelve college invitations in hand, I met Don Schollander, home from college for a visit with the members of the Santa Clara Swim Club. Don was a couple of years ahead of me in school and had been swimming at Yale University since 1965. He had won eleven AAU titles. In 1963, Don became the first swimmer in history to break two minutes in the two hundred-meter freestyle. Just four months after he graduated from

Santa Clara High School, he won four gold medals and set three world records at the 1964 Olympic Games.

Don stopped by the pool to watch the team swim. I had just finished a race and, even before I could get out of the water, Don kneeled on the pool deck and reached out his hand to greet me and congratulate me on my recent successes.

"Why don't you come to Yale, Fred, and swim with me?" he asked. That fall, he would start his senior year as the captain of the swim team. I was flattered at the invitation and a little in awe at the idea of attending an Ivy League school in Connecticut. I was intrigued—for a minute or two.

But then I reflected on the memory of my frozen feet in the snow up at the top of Haleakala when I was a boy.

No way! I thought. A cold climate held no appeal for me. I wanted to stay on the West Coast with easy access to the ocean, with never a flake of snow.

I gratefully acknowledged Don's offer, explaining why I would decline his generous invitation.

I spent a few days checking out the swimming programs at USC, UCLA, UC Berkeley, and Stanford.

None of the schools were as nice as Stanford. It was only an hour from Santa Clara where I had friends, and it was near the ocean where I could surf. I especially liked the swimming coach, Jim Gaughran. He coached the Stanford swim team from 1960 to 1980, training twenty-six Olympic swimmers who set twenty-six world records. His Stanford team had just completed their best meet, winning the NCAA Swimming Championship at Michigan State University. His swimmers swam lifetime best performances and broke records. Stanford's eight hundred-free relay beat the American record by an unbelievable 8.1 seconds.

I liked Jim. (I still do!) I was eager to join his team.

Ranked as one of the top universities in the world, Stanford was likened to a West Coast Ivy League school, with challenging academics and stringent admission standards.

The dozen scholarship offers I had received from colleges who wanted me to come to swim with them were just invitations. They weren't offers of admission. I didn't know if I could get into those schools with my low test scores and my solid B-minus grades.

So Stanford was my choice, and it was among the schools that invited me to apply. They asked me to retake the Scholastic Aptitude Test to see if I could raise my scores. My math score went up two hundred points, bringing the average high enough to be considered for admission.

But my score on the verbal portion of the exam was still pretty pitiful. It was so low that the dean of admissions asked to meet with me. That invitation had me a little worried. My high school counselor told me I was wasting my time applying to Stanford.

I walked into his very dark and gloomy office. On his desk were a leather desk mat and one of those lamps with a green shade that shone just a little bit of light right on what he was reading. A foot-high stack of files sat on either side of that spot. The bookshelf behind him was full of all sorts of leather-bound books. I had ever seen anything like that office before.

I stood before the desk in that intimidating office and looked down like a supplicant at the man sitting before me. I'm very tall, so I towered over him.

"Well, Fred," he said, leaning back in his chair, crossing his arms over his chest, and looking up over his half-rimmed glasses at me. "Jim Gaughran says you can swim quite well, but I have one question. Can you speak English?"

He was serious.

It was everything I could do to not roll my eyes or be insulted. Instead of getting angry, I took a breath and chose to have a little fun with him.

I have learned that in adversity, if you can laugh, you can get through any disagreement. I couldn't defend my low verbal aptitude test. I had probably read five or six books in my life outside of school. I was limited in my vocabulary, limited in my comprehension, limited in my reading skills. I couldn't argue with that. I figured humor in this instance was my only option. So I went with it.

"Yes, sir, I can speak English very well," I told him. "My parents speak English. My friends speak English. But..."

"You know da guys I wen go school wit, they never use da big kine word like I see on da SAT test. In da middle of da paragraph. So when I was doin da tes, ho, I look up. Everybody else stay readin. I stay stuck cuz I see a thirteen-letter word in da middle. So I just go'n mark any kine block. And I finish early, but no prize for finish early."

I paused to let it sink in. I rested my case.

"I'm bilingual. I speak English and Hawaiian pidgin. So just put me through bonehead English. I'll be out of your hair in four years."

Another pause. Then, the dean laughed. And I laughed.

Then I got serious. I assured him I intended to improve my verbal skills. I explained that my whole future was at stake, and I knew it. It was the reason I had left Maui to swim for Santa Clara. I wanted to attend Stanford. It was my ticket off the plantation. I was serious about completing my education in four years. I was serious about taking on the extra studying that might require. I was willing to work with my teachers outside of class. I would do whatever I needed to do. I was all in. I wanted to go to Stanford.

The dean of admissions looked at me deeply, taking a moment to assess what I had just told him. Then he smiled. He stood up and stepped around his desk to shake my hand and welcome me to the Stanford University Class of 1971.

I called my dad to tell him the good news.

"Dad! I got accepted!" I jumped right to the point. Remember, long-distance calls cost money. "I can get into Stanford and get a scholarship. I visited UCLA and USC and Berkeley. They all invited me to visit. I took the time to look at the campuses. But I think I would like to go to Stanford. Can you just sign the financial disclosure?"

"What do you mean?" Dad asked.

"Well, if you fill out a paper I'll send you, I can get a scholarship."

"What are you saying, Fred? They want to ask a lot of questions about what I have and what I make and what I own?"

"Yeah, I guess," I replied. "It's just a standard two-page form. Fill it out, and we'll get a scholarship!"

My dad would have none of it.

"It's none of their business what I have and what I own! Why don't you just go to Stanford, if that's where you want to go. I'll pay for it. That scholarship can go to someone who needs it."

That was my dad. He may have been stingy with his praise, but he was generous with just about everything else—including his commitment to seeing the best in me even when I could not.

From First to Failing

Everything about Stanford was a challenge—well, everything except swimming. I had friends to swim with, and I felt at home in the pool. Coach Gaughran welcomed me warmly. We still speak occasionally—fifty years later—like the good friends we are, remembering the good times we enjoyed.

Away from the pool, Stanford was intimidating. I know most college freshmen experience a challenging adjustment to college life until, say, the end of the first semester. It took me a couple of years to settle in comfortably.

At first, I was lonely, but I never stay lonely for long. My first friend outside the swim team was my roommate, Jeff Spann, from New Jersey. We laughed about the way we talked. I said "water," and he said *wahtah*. I paid close attention to the way he spoke. He was so smart, and his vocabulary was much larger than mine. If you don't have a strong vocabulary, you can miss just a word or two and you won't understand what people are saying.

"Would you please just speak simply to me?" I asked Jeff. "I've got a lot of work to do to catch up to everybody."

I even asked him to speak in five-letter words or less!

The students at Stanford were all smart, coming with straight As on their high school records. After I turned in my first paper in English class, the teacher asked me to meet with him after class.

"What's this?" he asked.

"Well, I'm really trying hard," I told him. "I got this thesaurus. I'm trying to improve my vocabulary. I didn't have anyone to help me with it. I didn't know what I was doing. I tried to throw some big words in there."

"Well, we've got a lot of work to do," he said.

He doesn't know the half of it, I thought to myself. At least I didn't show off my pidgin!

My writing improved when another English teacher encouraged me to write from my heart. That helped me learn to let the words flow and then go back later to work on my vocabulary. I've got a pretty good heart, so the papers improved, and my confidence increased.

Then there was math. I have always been good at math. But, of course, Stanford challenged me again, as I was taking calculus and analytic geometry for the first time. My good heart and fluency in pidgin couldn't help me at math.

I studied pretty hard, and I thought I had it until I went to take my first test. I read the first question. I read the second question. I read the third question. There were only three questions on the exam! I didn't know what the teacher was asking. I didn't get the gist of the long questions. Once again, my insecurity about my limited vocabulary stopped me. I tried to complete the exam as best I could, but I knew I was off course.

It wasn't until I walked out the door of the classroom that it dawned on me. I knew what to do. I had the answers. I put so much emotional and psychological pressure on myself to do well, I froze.

I got an F on my first math test. I failed my first writing assignment. Sure, I had been a B-minus student, but never an F student.

My Stanford career wasn't off to a good start. Part of me wanted it to be over.

I called my dad after being in college four weeks.

"Dad, I think I want to come home."

"What's that?" Dad asked. "Like, take some time off?"

"Yeah, maybe take some time off."

"Why is that?"

"Well, I'm just having a hard time understanding everybody at school, and I'm doing poorly. My grades are terrible. My English teacher had a meeting with me after class, and I flunked my first math test. I just think maybe I ought to take a break."

"Well," Dad replied, "you've got the rest of your life to decide to quit. Why don't you just give it two weeks and call me back?"

That was enough of a compromise for me.

I aired it out to the scariest person I could tell. Rather than say, "no, you cannot leave. I demand you to stay there," he encouraged me to stick with it. Dad gave me a chance, essentially, to stay there. That was just like him—he would give me enough rope to hang myself or climb out.

Two weeks wasn't long, and it was long enough. It was exciting in a way that anyone who has faced a monumental trial understands. An opportunity that was both challenging and humbling confronted me—a kind of "come-to-Jesus" understanding. I needed to pull it together. So I ramped up my commitment and worked harder than ever.

I went to the library every night after dinner and studied till ten o'clock. I would get up at four-thirty in the mornings and start studying again. I had more books to read in the first quarter of my freshman U.S. History class than I had read in my life. (Well, maybe that's an exaggeration, but it sure seemed like it. Those books were thick!) I was a slow reader, and I may have had attention deficit disorder. But my diligence paid off. By the end of the first year at Stanford, I probably tripled or quadrupled my reading speed.

I brought the same attitude to improving my academic skills as I brought to competitive swimming. To fly high, I knew to hang out with eagles in their nests. Mark Spitz flew higher than anyone; hanging with him and his family in their nest benefited my swimming career. Stanford had no shortage of academic eagles. I made a point of becoming friends with other like-minded students in my classes that would study with me, starting with my roommate Jeff Spann, of course. Living with him was like living with a dictionary. My vocabulary grew quickly.

It took me two years to choose economics as my major. I considered business and applied to business schools. I was willing to consider graduate school if it would further my education. But when I heard an economics professor talk about the kind of jobs you could get with a business degree, I immediately abandoned that idea. It sounded so boring! I couldn't imagine myself in a coat and tie in a corporate environment. Studying economics was the path of least resistance, and it wouldn't put a lot of stress in my life. But being trapped in a suit would. I loved sand between my toes!

I also considered applying for a teaching credential. I thought I could be a good teacher. After I learned what teachers earned, I wasn't so encouraged.

Those failing grades had frightened me into improving. I studied when I wasn't in class or the pool, and it worked. My grades improved, and I settled comfortably into college life.

By my senior year, my academics were solid, and I felt some freedom to have a little fun again. Herb Mason and I were living in the boathouse on Stanford's Lake Lagunita and working as lifeguards for two dollars an hour. (Herb told me we only earned a buck and a quarter an hour. He's probably right, since the minimum wage in 1970 was a $1.60.)

Campus protests against the Vietnam War were frequent, and they often grew violent. Herb and I and two of our buddies almost became victims one night when someone set our boathouse on fire while students burned down the ROTC building on campus.

Herb and I were asleep on the second floor, and two of our housemates were snoozing downstairs. Thank goodness I woke up when I heard someone walking around on the boathouse deck. It was about one in the morning. I heard a noise, like something tumbling over. We learned later that a protester rolled a motorcycle onto the deck. They opened the gas tank, pushed the bike over, and set it on fire. All of a sudden, my room lit up, and flames filled the window. I let out a huge scream, ran downstairs, banged on my roommates' doors, and woke everyone up. We put the fire out with an extinguisher. I hope whoever did it had no idea students were living there.

Aside from that scare, I was delighted with my digs. Living on the lake was fun. *Staying here is going to be great*, I thought. *I'm living right on campus, and I can get in the water*. Stanford gave Herb and me two thousand dollars to repair the rotten floating docks. I thought that was a dumb way to spend so much money, and I remember talking Herb into building a beach instead. I don't recall asking anyone for permission. We just hired a bulldozer to carve out a flat area along the lake. We brought in a dozen truckloads of sand and spread it around our new lakeside beach. The next week the beach was full of people sunning. Now we could lifeguard right on the beach. We were quickly the most popular guys on campus!

Today, Lake Lagunita is dry, and they tore down the boat-house. Herb tells me he did in fact get permission to build our beach! What a sad twist on a great memory.

Twenty Meters

A truly sad ending came for me in the pool.

During my freshman and sophomore years at Stanford, I swam for Jim Gaughran. We swam all year long, but during swim season, we had two grueling workouts a day. It seems like we were always tired. I was pushing it academically, too. If I wasn't in the library, I was in the pool. I wasn't in bed nearly long enough. But I was nineteen years old—stoked to win at school and in the pool.

And I did win in the pool. I was first in the one hundred-yard backstroke in both my freshman and sophomore years. In my sophomore year, we also won the four by one hundred medley relay at the NCAA competition. I won four NCAA gold medals and a silver medal in the Pan American Games.

I went back to Santa Clara in the summer of 1968 to train for the Olympics with George Haines. The workouts were tremendous. We were swimming five or six miles a day in short sprints. It was great to be back in the pool with Mark Spitz and to be challenged by the rest of George's top swimmers.

In late August, we headed to the Belmont Plaza Olympic Pool in Long Beach, California, for the Olympic trials. The technology for this competition was pretty exciting. These would be the first trials with electronic touchpads, timing, splits, and results boards.

I easily made it into the final qualifying race for my event—the hundred-meter backstroke. I slipped into the water and grabbed the edge of the pool, along with seven other guys, including Charlie Hickcox and Mitch Ivey. I knew it would be a close contest, but I felt appropriately confident when the gun went off.

I blocked out everything around me. I could imagine Mr. Spitz in my ear. *THERE IS ONLY ONE PERSON IN THE POOL!* In my mind, I was the only person in the pool.

I was dominating the race when I took the flip to make the turn. Twenty meters from the end, my body just slammed on its brakes. Everything went fuzzy, and the room started to spin. I had to *think* about what I was doing just to finish the race. I had to remember that my arms had to go over my head. I had to repeat the motion again and again and again until I reached the wall.

Oxygen wasn't flowing through my bloodstream. I didn't know it, but—just like a couple of years earlier in the Santa Clara pool—I had experienced an atrial flutter (or atrial fibrillation), when the heart's normal rhythm is out of whack. The heart can't keep up with the body's demands, and I was demanding a lot of it right then!

I was twenty meters from winning. My two teammates from Santa Clara passed me in the last twenty meters. I was twenty meters from swimming for the United States in the 1968 Olympics in Mexico.

But I ran out of gas, and I ended up in seventh place.

When I finally reached the wall, I was gasping for breath. It took a while for me to gather myself before I could even get out of the pool. Nobody asked what happened. Nobody wondered if something was wrong. Nobody called a doctor. I just lost. I thought I had over-trained. That's all there was to it.

That morning, I was number one in the backstroke in the nation. I tanked one race, and that's how my swimming career ended.

I thought, *Well, it's over now.*

I knew I had to shake off the disappointment.

I grabbed a buddy and said, "The waves are up. Let's go to Newport Beach and bodysurf the Wedge."

The Wedge, known for powerful, wedge-shaped waves at the tip of the Balboa Peninsula, has the biggest swell in Southern California. The waves can top thirty feet, and the backwash is so strong that new waves often crash into surfers trying to negotiate the wave they're riding. In summer and early fall, surfboards are too dangerous during the day—only bodysurfing is allowed.

Crowds come to watch those brave enough to take it on. Most locals have an appropriate respect for this piece of the ocean, and they wait a while before they consider venturing out. Not me—I was crazy enough to dive right in. I badly needed to discharge the pent-up energy from my swimming loss. Never mind that perhaps surfing was the last thing I should have been doing after my heart malfunctioned in the Long Beach pool.

The waves were huge—and brutal. Plenty of people were on the beach watching the few foolhardy swimmers willing to challenge the ocean that afternoon. I sauntered down to the water's edge in my tiny Speedo swimsuit, with no swim fins and my body totally shaved for the competition. I was quite the item on the beach that day!

I was a good bodysurfer, even without fins. But that day, the waves had their way with me. I dove beneath the first wave a little late. It broke right under me. It lifted me and threw me backward ten or fifteen feet onto the beach. I landed on my hands and knees. That had never happened to me before!

The waves were dangerous and mesmerizing. I stood up, walked back down to the water, and dove back in. I knew the ocean, and I refused to get beat again.

In tackling the Wedge, I felt the stoke! I turned a bad day into a better one.

The City of Flowers

swam at Stanford until I graduated in the spring of 1971, but once I missed the chance to compete in the '68 Olympics, I lost my passion for the sport. I still won a lot of races, even though I no longer swam double workouts or pushed myself. The 1972 Olympics would be the next significant challenge open to me, but what would I do for the year after graduation as I trained for the possibility of making the Olympics? I was surprised to find that I had no interest in going. I had made it to the top of the swimming ranks. After that first exciting win, the others became routine.

Most of my buddies at Stanford had started swimming when they were children—eight or younger. They still had strong aspirations and support from family and friends. I had no one driving me on. Mr. Spitz had done just that—in a shockingly effective way—one night at his dinner table. Now I was on my own. I was driving my future. I had accomplished my swimming aspirations. I had achieved success beyond my expectations. I didn't have to call my dad to know that he would advise me to look around to see what opportunity would show up next.

Getting a good education still was my top priority. Returning to work and life on Maui had been my goal ever since I managed to sidestep the drudgery of working on the chicken farm or in the pineapple fields.

So I turned my attention and my commitment to my studies. I had settled on economics as a major. For my final project, I evaluated the plans to develop tourism on Maui—in particular, an area on the south side of the island called Wailea. The proposed development was called The City of Flowers.

I wasn't the only one wondering what sort of work I would find when I returned home to Maui. Apparently, everyone was. Residents, business leaders, and government officials had been questioning how they could halt the exodus of people—young people, especially—to Oahu and the mainland after World War II, and the decline of employment in the sugar and pineapple industries.

The solution? Tourism.

Two significant events opened the way to developing Maui as a visitors' paradise: statehood in 1959 and affordable air travel. Oahu was experiencing an astounding influx of visitors, and the state government, local businessmen, and political leaders wanted to attract visitors to the outer islands.

One study, the "Report of Land Use for the Island of Maui," predicted the potential for Maui to grow a tourism industry:

> Maui is not fully utilizing its assets as a tourist attraction. As a result, it is missing an opportunity to obtain a rich source of revenue necessary to provide additional income and employment as an aid in maintaining not only its present population but to encourage future population growth. There are several fine sandy beaches in Maui [that] are on a par with the famous Waikiki Beach. ... The only thing that stands in the way of expanding the visitor in-

dustry is the ability to (1) persuade the people to vacation in Maui and (2) to accommodate them if they come. [1]

Nobody was more acquainted with those "fine sandy beaches in Maui" than I was, who had swum and surfed every one of them since I was old enough to cling to a surfboard. The idea of a giant influx of people to my remote island home confounded me, prompting me to take on the proposed development of Wailea as my senior project.

Ten years earlier, on the west side of the island, Ka'anapali pioneered the concept of a resort destination. The first in Hawaii, it was a planned development—hotels, restaurants, shopping, golf, and, of course, beaches—to meet all the needs of visitors, all within walking distance. First, they built the Royal Lahaina in 1962. The Sheraton and the Ka'anapali Beach Hotel were built in 1964, and then the Maui Surf Hotel. A lot of celebrities bought private homes at the Royal Lahaina. You never had to leave once you got there. That was an excellent plan for two reasons. Ka'anapali was hours from the airport, and there was nothing else on the island to do—yet.

When I was growing up, Ka'anapali was sugar fields, a big kiawe forest, and a feedlot. I could not understand why tourists would want to stay near that!

We would have birthday parties at the Cliff House, past Ka'anapali near Kapalua. The Cliff House was just that—a house built on a cliff at the edge of Namalu Bay, where the managers of the Honolua Plantation hung out in the 1940s. We would jump off the cliff and swim over to a little rocky island. It was danger-

---

1   Community Planning, Inc. and R.M. Towill Corporation. July 1959. *Report of Land Use for the Island of Maui.* Prepared for County of Maui, Planning and Traffic Commission. Wailuku, Maui.

ous to clear the edge of the rocks, but we were kids, and we didn't know any better. I guess our folks didn't either. This was back in the days of family parties. Getting to that part of the island was a long drive, and sometimes we would spend the night.

The west side offered beautiful beaches and romantic views of the islands of Lanai and Molokai. The little town of Lahaina was just down the road, with its charming old shops and bars. And there was water—West Maui is one of the wettest places in the world.

So Ka'anapali offered the proof of concept for success of the resort destination model and set a precedent for development across the island. Maui's population and economy began to grow. Over the next couple of decades, tourism became Maui's primary industry, impacting the island's population, infrastructure, economics, and even its culture.

After Ka'anapali, developers turned their ambitions to Kapalua and Wailea.

Even in 1970, Wailea—now the exotic, desirable, and pricey mecca for Maui tourism—was a desert with no infrastructure, and no water. Water came from Ulupalakua Ranch in a three quarter-inch line down to the beach. People joked that if one family turned on their lawn sprinklers, nobody else in the neighborhood had enough water pressure to take a shower. There was nothing in that hot, dry climate but scrappy kiawe trees, dirt roads, and lava rock. Less than a couple thousand people lived on the south side of the island. The only hotel, the Maui Lu, offered a hundred rooms.

The area's redeeming feature? *Beautiful* beaches.

Maui experienced a significant surge in tourism beginning in the late 1970s and continuing through the early 1990s, thanks in part to offshore investments. Mainland U.S. and Japanese companies built world-class resorts. The resident population bounced back, and immigration grew as the visitor industry filled the job vacancies created when the sugar industry was mechanized. United Airlines offered direct service from Los Angeles in 1983. In 1993 and for twelve more years, *Condé Nast Traveler* named Maui the "Best Island in the World." In 2000, more than two million visitors came to Maui from the mainland, the other Hawaiian islands, and other countries.

But I'm getting ahead of myself.

In the early seventies, less than fifty thousand people lived on the whole island, and a group of private developers funded the construction of a large, eighteen-inch waterline from the Wailuku aquifer to the desert-like south shore. A plan named "The City of Flowers" called for the construction of a vibrant, walkable, residential community, supported by tourism. It included shops, restaurants, hotels, apartments, and various attractions—including a Hawaiian antiquities museum—oriented around a flower-filled town square. Wailea would cater to tourists who wanted to escape the demands of city traffic. Cars would be restricted to the outskirts of town. Visitors and residents could get around on foot or in public shuttles. The population was projected to grow to fifty thousand, doubling that of the island at the time.

That plan was little more than discussions and drawings, and it was crushed when demands for condominiums escalated and prices soared. Anyone familiar with Wailea today knows it is a lush, luxury, resort community of fragrant tropical trees, great expanses of lawn, expensive luxury condos, and miles of roads to accommodate all the rental cars bringing tourists to the Grand Wailea, the Fairmont Kea Lani, the Four Seasons, and other posh hotels.

But, back in 1971, when I wrote my economics project on The City of Flowers and learned of the growth and opportunities developing on Maui, I knew only of the potential Maui offered me. I'd reached another one of my goals: I was on the verge of graduating from an excellent mainland university, and I was ready to return home and get to work.

I just had to figure out what that work would be.

A Process of Elimination

walked into Dad's office at the Maui clinic and handed him my checkbook. The checkbook had my name on it, but it was my parents' account. They had been paying my expenses while I was at Stanford, as my dad assured me he would do in lieu of my scholarship.

"Well, Dad, I'm finished with school," I said, stating the obvious. "Now what do I do?"

How many kids in the United States in those days were prepared—seriously prepared—to answer that question? Many were classically educated in such fields as English, education, history, psychology, and sociology, as were most who received traditional college educations at that time. I was a rarity with my economics degree—one of only fifteen thousand bachelor's degrees awarded in 1971 in the U.S—but I wasn't trained for a *job*.

I had completed four years at Stanford, the equivalent of an Ivy League university, earning a degree in economics. I won athletic championships at the highest levels. Well, short of the Olympics, of course. I was twenty-two years old. I'd accomplished all that was expected of me, and some things that surprised everyone— including me.

Now, I was home on a large island with a population the size of a small town. I'd gotten a good high school education; I had excelled at a sport, I earned a college degree. And for what? I didn't know what to do next. So, I came to the only person I knew whose counsel I would trust.

The conversation with my dad was significant—in part because of the advice he gave me, but more because of what he would share with me about himself.

"Well, son," he said, "I've been a doctor pretty much all my life. And I'm not sure it's what I wanted to do. I always thought being a marine biologist might be more exciting, and here I am being a doctor."

It never occurred to me that he had considered any other profession. His work was highly regarded and very much needed. I knew that from the frequent house calls he made at night. Dad was a pillar of the community. His calm, matter-of-fact demeanor was respected. He was always giving.

"Oh, sure, being a doctor has given me a lot of satisfaction. I help people, and I make a difference. But you're also subject to death, and you feel the emotions of patients' families. Having to explain to a family when a loved one dies is not easy, and it hurts."

That got my attention. Dad never revealed his personal feelings with us kids.

He paused and looked at me, thinking. I had been in California for five years, and I had the sense that he was sizing up how to address this young man sitting in his office.

"Fred, your job is just to get busy with whatever you want to do right now," he said. "You can be a garbage man, you can be a waiter, you can work construction, what have you. Just learn to do the best with the highest regard to quality in the business that you're in."

So, no big revelations there. He had, more or less, just listed all the jobs on the island. (At least he didn't tell me to apply at the chicken farm.) And, it was second nature for me always to do my best.

What came next would give me a whole lot of freedom, and I don't think I am exaggerating to say it shaped my worldview.

"Pretty soon, you might find yourself not so excited about it anyway," Dad continued. "And you'll want to move on. So, move on. That's it. You move away from what you don't want to do. Why? Because you're not moving toward what you want to do."

Was Dad setting me up to be a quitter? Was he suggesting I should leave a job just because I didn't like it? No. His was a question he had asked me often: *Is this what you want to do?* But only now was he articulating its import.

I realize Dad had just validated my decision to stop swimming. I had become a champion swimmer. The day I lost the qualification for the Olympics, I decided to move my attention elsewhere. I didn't quit. Haywoods aren't quitters. But I began to look for what was next. Dad was ahead of his time. Now, nearly fifty years later, students in a class at Stanford (and a book) called "Designing Your Life" start to figure out what they want to do by trying different things, expecting to change careers a few times.

I say life is a process of elimination. Just like you clean your house at times to clear out the stuff you aren't using, I believe in letting go of activities that no longer interest you, expectations that no longer serve you, even relationships that demand more time than you're willing to give. Just get rid of them. And yes, I've learned you can quit a job that isn't fulfilling, for any reason.

Designing My Life

n the summer of 1971, my options for work were in the sugar or pineapple fields or at one of the new hotels opening up. Working in the fields wasn't an option, of course. That's why I went to college—to avoid that fate. The other options were slim.

That's how I found myself, a recent Stanford University graduate, working as a busboy at the QueeQueg restaurant in the brand-new Maui Surf Hotel on Ka'anapali Beach. I was determined to do my best—and have fun.

The fun part, of course, was surfing. I was surfing in Honolua Bay with my buddy Bill Boyum and his brother Mike and hearing their stories about surfing in Bali. Bali was surfing's best-kept secret. Mike was planning to establish a surf camp there and introduce it to the world. I wanted nothing more than to go to Bali for a few weeks to discover the awesome waves in Indonesia before the floodgates opened. I just had to figure out how to pay for the plane ticket.

Before long, I advanced to being a waiter at the QueeQueg. One night, I was clearing a table and had placed the plates on a tray to take them back to the kitchen. Suddenly, the tray flipped upside down. The plates landed on the floor with a crash and, of course, broke. The manager of the restaurant became very angry, calling me a "dumb busboy," even while the restaurant was filled with people. Well, I wasn't a busboy. I had been a waiter for a year, and, I was pretty sure I wasn't dumb. So I figured that it was probably a good time for me to move onto something else.

That turned out to be construction.

With so many resorts going up on Maui, it wasn't hard to find a job, and I was young and fit. For several months, I worked as a laborer on a new resort in Napili. Every morning around six, I would leave my house in Kahului, jump in the back of a truck with some buddies, drive about an hour over to Napili, and return with others around three-thirty in the afternoon.

The work was hard, but it was outdoors, and I was pretty content. That is, until I met the realtor selling condos.

Each morning, I noticed a guy stroll up to the front door of the building I was working on. He'd show up at about nine-thirty, wearing an aloha shirt and slacks and carrying a folding chair, a newspaper, and his coffee. He would sit outside the door, enjoying the sun and sipping his coffee, until someone came along. I couldn't always hear what was being said, depending on the racket of the construction equipment we were using, but I'd notice him talking with folks a bit. Sometimes I'd see them walk into the building, exiting fifteen or thirty minutes later. I was kind of jealous—but mostly curious. He wasn't coming to work at seven-thirty in the morning like I was, and he wasn't doing hard labor.

One day, I was three stories up on some narrow scaffolding, working on the wall of a new building. Rebar stuck out of the wall, and I was filling the holes with cement. I was in a pretty precarious spot. I had no safety lines; I just clung to the rebar as I moved along the wall and pumped cement from a grout hose coming from the cement truck on the street. I wasn't afraid—maybe I didn't know I should be.

A couple came to the entrance and chatted with the guy, whom I had come to know by this time. After what seemed just five minutes, they walked out again. The realtor shook their hands, saying, "Okay, you bet. I'll get that done." I knew he had sold a condo. After the couple left, I hollered down from the scaffolding.

"How much was that one?" I asked.

"That'll bring me an eighteen hundred-dollar commission," he replied.

That got my attention. I was working for five dollars and twenty-five cents an hour. I figured it would take me the rest of the summer to earn eighteen hundred bucks... let alone save that much.

"That's it," I said to myself. "I'm getting out of construction. I'm going to go get my real estate license."

Straight after I got off work that afternoon, with splatters of cement on my work clothes and my face, I headed to see my friend Bob Cole, who worked in a real estate office near my home.

"Hey, Bob," I said. "How do I get into this business?"

He told me a class had just started. It met on Saturdays at Baldwin High School. I had missed the first one, but I should go to the next one anyway.

"Just tell them you'll catch up," Bob said.

So I did.

A Cosmic Wave with Gerry Lopez

Bill Boyum lived with me and my brother Jimbo in the house we grew up in. By this time, my folks had moved to nicer digs, leaving us the house near the harbor in Kahului. The three of us had a great time, as single guys in their twenties do so well. The house was hidden behind a jungle of vegetation, and it was showing its age. But it was our "Animal House." We put a ping-pong table in the huge living room. Jimbo would bring home giant slabs of ahi tuna from some fishermen he knew. We had a bandsaw set up in the house, and we'd use it to slice up the fish. We were fit from eating all that fish and surfing the big waves at Pier One, just a few blocks from the house.

Bill talked all the time about his surfing adventures in Bali.

"When are you going again?" I asked. "Because I want to go with you."

And I wanted to go as soon as I could. I knew real estate was my ticket, so to speak, because I could earn some serious money. The day after I met with Bob Cole, I started the real estate course. A few months later, I had my license. About six months after that, I closed my first sale—a new A-frame house on two acres upcountry in Kula. It sold for under a hundred thousand dollars, and I made around two percent commission. I sold a property in Maui Meadows, near Kihei, next.

My long-term plan was to work three months and surf for six. I figured selling real estate eventually would give me the means to do that. Sure enough, as a brand-new Realtor, in about six months I had earned enough money to pay for a trip to Indonesia.

In May 1974, I bought a plane ticket and headed to Bali for two months with Bill Boyum.

We headed first to Kuta where we rented a house on the beach for a dollar a night. Massages were two dollars. Beers were the most expensive—a couple of bucks each. We surfed for forty-seven of the sixty days I was there, five or six hours a day. Life was good.

Today, surfers consider Indonesia to have some of the finest surfing conditions on the planet. The winds blow offshore every day—the smoothest water comes with straight, offshore winds blowing out over the ocean—and perfect waves run along the beach for twenty miles. Kuta today is a tourists' hotspot, especially for Australians, with plenty of bars, apartments, malls, hotels, stores, restaurants, traffic, and more surf stores per mile than anywhere else on the planet.

But when Mike discovered Kuta in 1970, it was a sleepy fishermen's village with beautiful beaches and cheap food and not a surfer in sight. Mike contacted Bill, telling him to fly over from Maui with surfboards.

Mike and Bill were surfing Bali when only a few knew about it. But word of the magnificent surfing was getting around. When filmmakers showed up to shoot the classic *Morning of the Earth*, Bill knew the secret wouldn't stay one for long.

After a few days of surfing at Kuta Beach where we were staying, Bill and Mike took me to Uluwatu. Uluwatu on the Bukit peninsula was still surfing's best-kept secret, even when I got there three years after the release of *Morning of the Earth*. Imagine the surface of the ocean with waves like wide-wale corduroy—rows of perfect peaks lined up all the way to the horizon, breaking left over the wide, shallow reef into the shore, one after the other, lined up evenly and producing clean barrels. When the tide is high, the surf is pretty mellow. Lower tides produce greater barrels.

But getting to Uluwatu from Kuta was a journey in itself. We hopped on little rented Suzuki motorcycles with our surfboards. We passed the airport and headed to Bukit on the southern tip of Bali. Here we found an awesome view a thousand feet below us to Jimbaran Bay and an ancient temple crawling with monkeys. We passed a couple of villages and some fields with cows grazing. Eventually, Mike stopped in what looked like the middle of nowhere. We parked our bikes in some vegetation, hidden from view from the side of the road, grabbed our gear, and set out for what Mike and Bill promised would be the best surfing day ever. I was stoked!

It wasn't an easy trek. It took us half an hour to get down to the beach, carrying our surfboards. The terrain was rough, and there was no clear path, but fortunately, Bill and Mike knew the way.

We traipsed along a hint of a trail through the jungle, negotiating a labyrinth of thorny cactus plants that grew like vines and that the locals sometimes used to fence their land. We scrambled through tangles of bamboo, passing some pastures with cows grazing. We trudged through more jungle for a while until we reached a drop. A makeshift ladder of vines and bamboo woven together took us down to a cave and the water. It was high tide, so the ocean nearly filled the cave. A pocket beach inside the cave provided a spot to stay dry and out of the sun.

From that little beach, we paddled out. The surf was phenomenal! We had the place all to ourselves—no surprise since the locals didn't surf. That day of surfing was the best I had ever experienced.

We hardly ever saw any people at Uluwatu on that trip—only monkeys in the jungle and the cows in the fields—until one morning about two weeks into the trip. We were halfway along the trek down to the cave when we saw three guys with surfboards ahead of us, slowing trudging their way on that zig-zag trail through the vegetation.

"Hey!" Mike hollered at them. They turned around, and even from the distance I could see surprise and relief on their faces—then huge smiles. They began waving like we were long-lost relatives and stopped to wait for us.

When we got closer, I thought they looked familiar.

"Oh, are we glad to see you!" one said. "I'm Jack McCoy, and these are my buddies Jeff Hakman and Gerry Lopez."

Gerry Lopez and Jeff Hakman were the two top surfers in the world.

For a minute, Mike and Bill looked a little stunned. They recognized these guys, too, of course. I'm never at a loss for words, so I made the introductions.

"Well, I'm Fred Haywood," I said. "This is my buddy Bill Boyum and his brother Mike."

We all shook hands. I felt like I was meeting a couple of celebrities.

"We're from Maui. Are you guys over from Oahu?" I asked.

I quickly realized that was a dumb question. I knew very well where they were from. I'd been following their surfing careers for a while. These guys were beyond thrilled to find anybody that day—we could have been from Maui or from Mars. They were elated to see us because they were lost, and it looked like they had been for a while.

"We're looking for a beach called Uluwatu," Jack said. "I thought I knew where it was, but now I can't find the way. I know there is a way to get down the cliffs, but how?"

Gerry, Jeff, and Jack had been walking for an hour and a half trying to find the way down to the Uluwatu beach. They were hot, sweaty, and bug-bitten. They were surprised to meet fellow surfers from Hawaii, of all places. They were deeply grateful to finally encounter folks who could get them to that elusive Ulu surf. No wonder we all became fast friends. We led the way to what had been our private playground, elated to finally be able to show it off to guys who would dig it like we did.

When they scrambled down the ladder into the sea cave, they encountered the magnificent surf. Gerry said it looked like the gateway to paradise. And we had it all to ourselves.

I was pretty stoked to surf with other guys, and surfing with two world champs like Gerry and Jeff was a bonus! It couldn't have been a more magical day on the water. We didn't have to worry about crowds of people hanging around to watch these superstars, like we would have had we been in Hawaii. I wasn't even close to being on their level, but that didn't matter. The ocean is the great equalizer, especially in a new spot like Uluwatu. We were all figuring it out together.

It was great synergy. We all had a great time surfing that day. We became good friends, and we surfed together every day after that while we were in Bali. We didn't always go down to Ulu. It was a challenge, even for seasoned pros like Gerry and Jeff. Some days, we'd just take it easy on Kuta Beach right outside our front door, enjoying cheap massages and a few beers at the end of the day.

One afternoon, Gerry and I decided to head down to Ulu on our own. It was late in the afternoon, and when we got down the ladder to the cave we found half a dozen Australians who had been surfing all morning. The waves were good size, but the wind was blowing straight onshore, hitting us in the face pretty fiercely. The surface was lumpy, so the surf wasn't very good.

Gerry and I decided to go surfing anyway and make what we could of the few hours we had before dark. We paddled out of the cave, drifting a couple hundred yards down before we could get out with the current where the waves washed through. Once we got out of the break, I turned around to see the Aussies leaving, walking up the hill. Just then, the wind changed, and I felt the offshore breeze hit me in the face. All of a sudden, Gerry and I had a perfect Uluwatu incoming tide. I knew that for the next two or three hours, it was going to be really good.

Gerry Lopez had won three major surf contests in a row. I was feeling pretty blessed to be surfing with the best surfer in the world. I was not a competitive surfer like he was. I was just a playful surfer, and here I was surfing alone with him.

We were surfing the inside section when the wind suddenly turned offshore. For a surf to be good, a lot of things have to happen. The wave has to line up. The wind has to be right; the swell has to be separated. All of a sudden, all the angles were perfect. The tides were perfect. The wind was perfect.

Now the waves were starting to tube, and we were getting a lot of tube rides. I remember him taking the first wave of a particular set, and then I could see outside that there were some bigger waves. I took the third one. I paddled deeper than I'd ever paddled and turned around and took off. It was what we would call a "six-foot Hawaiian," a wave with a ten-foot face—or taller.

As I was dropping in, the lip was in front of me, coming down with me. It was already pitching in front of me, where I wanted to go. So, before I met the bottom of the wave, I pushed on a rail to cut to the left hand, and I backdoored that tube. In other words,

I went into a tube ride from the "back door," rode a good six or seven seconds inside, and pushed up onto the nose to make it.

I can remember being unable to see anything. Inside the tube, all I could hear was rumbling of *whoa, whoa, whoa, whoa* … and all of a sudden—I came out! I was bent so far forward at the waist my body almost turned around backwards.

When I came out of the tube, I fell right in front of Gerry.

"Oh my God!" Gerry hollered at me. "That was the longest tube ride I've ever seen backside anywhere! I couldn't even see you in the tube!"

"Yeah, I was in all the wash," I said in amazement. "I was just in the wash and holding on for life."

That's not an exaggeration. Gerry named the inside section "The Racetrack" for the high-speed, full-throttle runs. We were risking our lives. I didn't want to think about what would happen if we fell into the razor-sharp reef below. We surfed for another hour that day. For me, that rush with one of the best surfers in the world was nothing less than a cosmic experience.

A Suitcase Full of Puka Shells

Until they started surfing at Uluwatu, Gerry and Jeff had never used surf leashes. If they fell, they were skilled enough to hang onto their boards. But Ulu's rocky shoreline would smash up a board pretty quickly if it got away from you. We had brought our boards with us, so losing one was costly. Not in money, but in being short a surfboard—we couldn't replace it.

In those days, surfboard leashes were made of a length of nylon encased in stretchy surgical tubing, the kind a nurse uses to wrap a tourniquet around your arm to check your blood pressure. If you fell off the board, the tubing would stretch, the nylon would stop it, and the flexible tubing would rebound, snapping your board back.

But sometimes the waves at Ulu pulled so hard on the leash that the nylon would break. The tubing would keep stretching until it broke, too, or recoiled, slamming the board back. It could be downright dangerous. You were busy coming up for air after a tumble in the waves—the last thing you needed was your board flying toward your head at supersonic speed.

Jeff soon gave up on the leash, preferring to concentrate on never losing his board. But one day, Mike dumped right in front of him, and Jeff had to let go to avoid a collision. The board was swept away with waves. We all took a break from surfing to find it—that's what we did in those days. Surfing might be a solitary sport, but it was also one of solidarity. We all paddled down the coast, looking to see if it had washed up anywhere. We never found the board, but I found what would turn out to be, for me, a fortune in puka shells.

Puka is Hawaiian for "hole." A puka shell is a cone-shaped snail shell broken down so much that a hole is worn in the cap. You can string them all together to make leis or puka shell necklaces.

Puka shells in the sixties were iconic to surf culture. Then, David Cassidy of *The Partridge Family* fame introduced them to the world, wearing white puka shell chokers everywhere, even on TV and during his concerts. My sister, Anne, who owned a shop on Front Street in Lahaina, told me puka shell necklaces were incredibly popular, and the shells were worth a lot of money.

These necklaces were a fashion trend that had yet to arrive in Bali. So, when I stumbled onto that beach in search of Jeff's surfboard, I was thrilled to find it covered in puka shells. A few days before I would return home to Maui, I brought a couple of Balinese guys to the beach. I paid them fifty cents a kilo to collect as many shells as they could. They loaded me up with about twenty kilos of the shells. I paid them ten dollars and carried them home on the plane. My Pan Am bag was so heavy the handles broke.

When I returned to Maui, I started stringing those shells into necklaces and sold them for nearly fifty bucks a strand. That's how I made money until I could sell another house.

G-Land

A round 1970, Bill Boyum discovered a place in Indonesia called Grajagan, on the southern part of Java. It literally was off the beaten path. Grajagan, or G-Land, is a long stretch of coral reef bordering the last remaining patch of Javanese jungle.

Mike Boyum's buddy Bob Laverty was flying to Java in 1971 when he experienced a bit of serendipity. A storm diverted his flight over the south coast. Bob looked out the window of the plane and noticed a colossal wave off a peninsula jutting like a nose into the Indian Ocean.

Determined to find it, he went back a year later with Bill. Accessing the peninsula through the jungle was as challenging as getting to Uluwatu. Schlepping surfboards, Bill and Bob took a couple of fat-wheeled Suzuki 80 motorcycles through Bali, over the ferry, and across Java. Then they put their bikes in some small canoes to cross to the peninsula. They rode down to the point to find the surf. The trek was worth it to find the most beautiful barrel waves they had ever seen. Bill Boyum and Bob Laverty had just discovered G-Land—the best surf in the world.

Eventually, Mike would establish the first surf camp there. It was primitive—not unlike the book *Robinson Crusoe* he had read when he was a kid. Bill and Mike built a camp for about ten people. Everyone slept in bamboo treehouses, safe above the tigers that roamed through the camp at night. They kept their food in Igloo ice chests. Boats brought ice, vegetables, and chicken. Campers would catch fish for their dinner.

After my cosmic wave experience with Gerry, I ran into some friends who wanted to surf G-Land. They said they would be gone for nine days, and they would sail there. They asked me, did I want to go?

Of course I did!

Mike Ritter, Bob Jones, Bob Pritikin (the son of Nathan Pritikin, the diet doctor who pioneered treating heart disease with a healthful diet and exercise), and I headed out to find what were supposed to be the best waves in the world. None of us had been there, and we didn't know where to go. So, we headed to the tip of Java and a large game preserve filled with tigers, orangutans, six-foot monitor lizards, and other creatures on a trimaran that a friend had abandoned in the Kuta harbor. A trimaran is a boat with a main hull and two smaller, outrigger hulls. Ours had bunks to sleep in, and it was large enough to walk through the cabin without bending over. It was very comfortable. We didn't have any refrigeration, so we just ate peanut butter we brought with us and fish we caught.

We moored the sailboat about a quarter-mile from the shore. When we woke up the next morning, we saw two- and three-foot waves about a hundred yards from the boat. It was awesome, and it kept getting better. The next day, we surfed six- and eight-foot waves. Every day I thought I had surfed the best day of my life. And then I would wake up and do it again.

I would catch a wave and kick out, only to find another section right in front of me. I would paddle over a little bit to catch it and go a long way, and then kick it out. And there would be another section in front of me! So I'd catch that and go to another section. The winds were coming straight offshore at five miles an hour, making the waves so crisp and clean.

By the ninth day, everybody was surfed out, so the guys took the little Zodiac inflatable boat over to the beach for the day. But the waves were just perfect again, and I didn't want to stop. So I paddled out by myself and surfed for hours in what I thought was the best surf I'd ever had.

Imagine. I was three-quarters of a mile off a remote island, all by myself, with no village around for thirty miles—just a game preserve with orangutans and tigers and things in the jungle alongside the beach. Killer whales passed me a ways out, and sharks swam in the lagoon. But I had no fear. After so many days in the water, I was in tune with nature. I experienced a surreal sensation of being one with the environment.

And the waves just kept coming. They were easily eight feet, maybe ten or twelve, if you measured the face of the wave. They just wouldn't stop!

Oh, I thought, *that was the best wave of my life!* Then I'd paddle back out and go deeper. *Oh, my god, no. THAT was the best wave!*

I picked up five waves in a row that were the best five waves I ever had. They just wouldn't stop. My last one was a phenomenal ride. I was on my board, and, instead of riding crouched over, I stood straight up. I was maybe fifteen feet deep, riding in the tube with my body upright and my hands straight up in the air. I've never experienced another wave quite like that. Whether it was the water itself, my developing skill, or just the otherworldly, mindless state I was in, it was as if everything just stopped. The world disappeared around me while I was riding that wave. I was absolutely in the moment and in eternity at the same time. It was indescribable and nothing short of unbelievable.

It was much like the day Gerry and I had surfed alone, one of those cosmic experiences, but this time all by myself.

After that, I was done. I was ready to go home. I had achieved everything I wanted to. I rode the best wave of my life, and it happened on the last day, surfing the most exceptional waves on the planet. A day later, I packed up my gear and my puka shells and hopped on a plane home to Maui.

Three Months On, Six Months Off

Those puka shells kept me in groceries until I could sell another house. I came back to work for a real estate company in Kihei. Puka shell necklaces were selling for around forty-five dollars a strand. That was a lot of money in 1973, so I sat in the office and strung enough puka shell necklaces in a few months to make a couple thousand dollars. (That was about as much as I earned in commission when I sold my first property in upcountry Kula. I discovered quite a treasure on that beach in Bali!)

Eventually, my real estate work paid off, too. I was able to work for two or three months and earn enough money to go surf for half a year. I surfed Costa Rica, El Salvador, Mexico, and Tahiti. I went back to surf California and Indonesia, too.

A most peculiar event happened to me while surfing in El Sunzal, El Salvador. I was sharing a home about a hundred yards from the beach with several other surfers and random travelers. My bed was a hammock hanging from the ceiling upstairs in an open-air space. Early one morning, another surfer, Bernie Baker from Oahu, whom I had met in the home, walked with me down to the beach. We headed into the ocean with our surfboards. He and another friend were in front of me by about two hundred feet, paddling out on top of the silky smooth morning water to the surf spot.

I looked up to see they had startled three sixteen-foot-wide manta rays! Two took off for the horizon. The third one turned and headed directly my way. Water flowed over its head like a submarine skimming the surface, and I could see that the sides of its mouth were wider than my surfboard. I grabbed my surfboard rails to hold on as it passed directly under my board. The water all around me went black. All of a sudden, both wings lifted out of the water and smacked each other well over my head, while its shoulders touched mine ever so delicately. The wings encircled me, creating a tunnel, while water sprayed down on me. It was a surreal, almost magical encounter.

"Are you okay?" Bernie screamed.

"Yes!" I yelled back. "I just got the first tube of the day! WHOO-HOO!"

I felt I had been blessed and refreshed with the tube, shower, and incredible experience.

Thank goodness real estate was lucrative, because I wanted more of that magic on the water.

I followed the model of my "mentor"—the guy who opened my eyes to the potential of real estate when I was working construction, only with a twist. I rented a unit in a popular condo complex and an office on the ground floor. I advertised the condo at a high price and sat outside, waiting to show it to prospective customers. When folks came to see it, they would naturally balk at the price. So I'd pick up my for-sale signs and show them other properties. It turned out to be a pretty savvy way to get leads.

I could earn enough working three months a year to travel for the next six months. I was in my twenties, and I didn't see how life could get any better.

Then I discovered windsurfing.

In 1979, I was living in the Whaler, a condominium complex in front of the Sheraton in Ka'anapali. My unit overlooked the beach. One morning I looked out the window to see, coming from the north around the point called Black Rock, surfboards *with sails!* I could hardly believe my eyes—they were practically flying along the shoreline!

I dashed down to the beach to meet two guys who would turn into lifelong friends. Mike Waltze and Matt Schweitzer—now famous names in the windsurfing world—had just come to work at Ka'anapali beach to teach windsurfing.

Mike and Matt had set up a simulator on Ka'anapali Beach to teach folks how to windsurf before they got in the water. The simulator was a platform on golf balls. A sail was attached to the platform. A student would stand on the platform like they would a surfboard and hold onto a rod attached to the sail. The golf balls acted like ball bearings—every little move would shift the platform like a surfboard on water.

Once a student learned to manage the simulator, Mike and Matt had a pile of surfboards nearby to take them onto the water.

I jogged over to their makeshift classroom, where they were planting surfboards on end in the sand to serve as a billboard advertising their little school.

"Where did you guys come from?" I hollered when I got close enough to be heard over the surf.

"We came from Napili," one of them said, reaching out to shake my hand. "I'm Mike. Mike Waltze. This is my buddy, Matt Schweitzer. We teach windsurfing lessons here."

"You came from Napili?" I asked, incredulous. Napili was five or six miles up the coast. They had used the waves and the wind to sail down the beach.

Oh my gosh, I thought. *They avoided all the traffic! They came on their boards!*

"That's so amazing!" I said. "How are you going to get back?"

"Oh, we're just going to sail back," Matt said.

Back to Napili—*upwind.*

"I want to do that!" I said. "Will you teach me?"

I had planned to buy a small Prindle sailboat with a friend, but he had changed his mind. When I saw this new thing called windsurfing, I decided right then that I'd be putting surfing and sailing behind me to give it a go.

Little did I know how that seemingly small, impulsive pronouncement to no one but myself would shift my life in a radical new direction, and it was Mike who would show me the way.

Now, Mike tells the story of how we met a little differently:

"Every day, I would drag all my surfboards down to Ka'anapali Beach," Mike said. "I'd set up the simulator, and I would get ready to teach tourists how to windsurf all day.

"I could see you sitting in a chair at the front door of that condo where your office was. There you sat, under the shade, reading a book all day, like your life was perfect. Then one day, I left for a while, for some reason. When I came back, I noticed one of my sailboards was missing. I looked around to see you dragging it down to the beach.

"'Hey!' I hollered. 'What are you doing?'

"And you said, 'Well, I just wanted to try it. I've been watching you teach people for a week, and it looks so easy!'

"'First of all,' I told you, 'You don't just grab somebody's board and take it off the beach. If you want to learn, you need a lesson. Come here.'

"So, before you got to the water with my board, we dragged it back up the beach. I put you on the simulator, and I gave you a lesson.

"And that's how we met."

Mike tells the story that way to this day, and he says it definitively, leaving no room for doubt.

He may be right. However we met—and whether or not Matt was there that day—it was the first day of a lifelong friendship, years of awesome adventures on the water, and new careers in windsurfing.

Together, Mike and I evolved the sport and put the little island of Maui on the map as the windsurfing center of the world. That's a pretty bold thing for a guy like me to say, but it's the truth, and it all started when Mike Waltze introduced me to windsurfing.

Mike was nine years old when he started windsurfing in California with Matt, his best friend. Matt invented freestyle on a sailboard. He was the first one to play around in the waves and do tricks on a board. Matt's dad is Hoyle Schweitzer, who, with Jim Drake, essentially invented windsurfing. I say this with a load of caveats—who knows who first attached a piece of fabric to a board to fly across the surface of the water? But in 1969, Hoyle and Jim developed, patented, and marketed a device called a universal joint that connected the sail to the board, allowing the sail to rotate and control power and the board direction. Hoyle and his wife, Diane, had the passion to persevere through countless attempts to develop a working model. And it paid off—literally. A man from Seattle named Bert Salisbury saw Hoyle with the contraption and coined the term *windsurfer*. Hoyle and Diane saw the commercial possibilities and built a very successful company called Windsurfer International.

I couldn't get enough of this incredible experience of flying across the water, holding tight to a sail attached to a surfboard. Every afternoon when I closed up shop, I would walk down to Ka'anapali Beach and take one of Mike's sailboards out. At the end of the day, we'd enjoy a beer together and talk.

"I was driving to Hana the other day," Mike said to me one evening, "and I went past a beach called Ho'okipa. I want to sail there!"

Today the guidebooks call Ho'okipa Beach, on the north shore of Maui, a world-renowned windsurfing destination and the windsurfing capital of the world. Seventy percent of the time, the trade winds blow over twenty knots on Maui. The Pacific Ocean has the highest average wind flow. A suction, or venturi, pulls winds through the valley between the West Maui Mountains and Haleakala, creating powerful air flows parallel to the north shore coast. A reef runs three hundred yards to three-quarters of a mile along the shoreline, generating perfect waves. You can go to any spot along the north shore and get air and ride waves. But it's not an easy ride, especially for novices.

The day Mike said he wanted to go there, I tried to talk him out of it.

"You've got to get there early," I said, "because, after nine in the morning, it blows out."

"Well, that's what I want," Mike said. "I want the huge waves breaking outside and the howling, side-shore winds. I want to sail ninety degrees to the wind and ride waves. That's where I want to go sail, but I don't have a car."

When I offered to drive him over there for the day, he protested.

"No. I'm not in the right place. I need to *move* there." Napili, where he lived, was a two-hour drive from Ho'okipa. "I need to quit my job. I need to sail every day. I found a house. I've done the math. I need six thousand dollars. I found a car for nine hundred bucks. I can live on the rest for six months."

"What are you gonna do, Mike?" I asked. "How are you going to make a living? We have to work."

"I don't know, Fred. I'm just going to go sail every day. I don't know what's going to happen. But something's going to happen. Right now, I'm going to call my mom to see if she can help me."

"You don't need to call your mom, Mike," I said. "I'll co-sign a loan for you if you want to get a car. Let's go to the bank right now."

We went down to the Bank of Hawaii, where I co-signed a loan for Mike so he could get that car. In a couple of days, he was out sailing at Ho'okipa, and in six months, he had paid off the loan on the car.

Because, just as Mike predicted, something did happen. Wind-surfing was taking off in Europe, and equipment manufacturers were stepping up to fill the demand. They needed windsurfers to photograph for their advertisements. Because he didn't have a job and he wasn't in school, Mike was always available, so he got the gigs. He was eighteen years old and making five hundred dollars a day sailing for companies selling windsurfing gear. That was a lot of money for a kid in the late 1970s.

For twenty years, Mike, now a highly respected cinematographer, sailed for some of the best filmmakers in the world. His reputation grew, he was winning world windsurfing championships, and eventually, he was earning ten grand a month.

But for a while, Mike and I sailed all over the island. We'd sail Kanaha Beach until the wind died. We sailed Pier One, Outer Sprecks in front of the Maui Country Club, Lahaina Harbor, the Kihei boat ramp, and Honolua. We dodged lava rocks on the south side, sailing around the lighthouse at La Perouse and up the coast. We were pumped to windsurf every single day.

"Pumped" doesn't begin to describe the rush you get when flying across the water and through the waves on a board while holding on to a sail, especially at Ho'okipa. The sheer speed of the ride exponentially increased the challenge and the thrill over anything I had experienced on a surfboard. Having Mike to share the rush with was nothing less than awesome. When we had worn ourselves out at the end of a day on the water, we'd flop onto the sand with a cold beer and just sit together, without saying a word. The sensation was indescribable. How can you put words to magic?

Over the years of my participation in watersports, I had created special bonds with my teammates, whether it was Mark Spitz in the pool at Santa Clara or Bill Boyum and Gerry Lopez at Uluwatu. I sensed the same energetic connection with Mike. At that time, we had Ho'okipa all to ourselves, and that gave me a chance to wonder about it. Finally, I understood. We were generating and sharing endorphins together! When you share endorphins like that, you experience an enduring bond that is almost impossible to explain. That bond lasts a lifetime. I still can call up any of my buddies, and we connect like we had seen each other just yesterday.

Mike and I were stoked. We both could feel that something was poised for takeoff. Some sort of revolution was coming our way. We were waiting for a new idea to drop in.

Then my brother Jim was killed in a traffic accident.

Epiphany

I t was 1981, and real estate took a dive after the Federal Reserve raised interest rates to more than eighteen percent. Most folks were priced out of the market, and that trend would continue for several years.

Bill Boyum and I had gone separate ways for a while after our trip to Bali. He had moved upcountry to Kula, on the western slope of Haleakala, and taken up hang gliding. He was soaring from the summit of Haleakala about the time I was learning to windsurf. When we hooked up again, Bill was impressed with how fit I had become from the strenuous workouts I got sailing, so gave up hang gliding and took up windsurfing too. (It was much less risky, I assured him.) Living in Kula meant a long drive down to the beaches, so Bill soon moved into the Kahului house with Jim and me to be close to Kahana and Ho'okipa beaches.

Jim was working for Maui Oil, not far from the house or the harbor. When he would fill the tuna boats with fuel, he often scored a hundred-pound frozen ahi. He would bring the fish home, and right in the living room, we sawed it into steaks with a bow saw before tucking them away in the freezer. We enjoyed the motherload of sashimi, washing it down with beer. Jimbo would regale us with hilarious stories of his work encounters, and he could relate the various conversations perfectly in all the dialects heard on Maui: Chinese, Filipino, Japanese, and, of course, pidgin. It seemed like the three of us never stopped laughing.

When car lights lit up my bedroom late one night, I jumped out of bed to peer out the window. My bedroom was at the front of the house, well hidden from the street behind a dense growth of tropical plants. A car pulling into the driveway at night meant trouble. I saw Dad shuffling up the walk, head down and hands in his pants pockets. He never visited us, and especially not at midnight or one o'clock in the morning. I got to the door at the same time he did.

"Your brother's dead, son," Dad said. He was as calm as anyone might be who had too often experienced delivering such news in his career. "There was a head-on collision on the highway. Jimbo's gone."

I was in shock. But it was only the first of a one-two punch. I had just lost my brother. Two weeks later, I lost my livelihood.

I had been successful working real estate in Ka'anapali. I was selling properties, and I was buying them. I had invested in half a dozen properties on Maui, and I was making monthly payments on them from my real estate commissions. My three-months-on, six-months-off plan was working sweetly, until the real estate market cratered. Suddenly, I needed to find another way to make some money.

I asked around, and apparently, the money to be made at that time was in the stock market. I asked a friend who was a stockbroker how to get into that business.

"Fred," he said. "Look at you. And look at me."

He was all buttoned up in a suit and tie, and his skin was so white I assumed he never saw the sun. I, on the other hand, was fit and tan from windsurfing every day.

"I wish I looked like you," he said. "You are really healthy. Do you want to look like me?"

I did not.

"Oh," I said. "Yeah. I get it."

I had experienced an epiphany with Jim's death. Life was important, and I needed to live—and love—my life.

I did not want to become a stockbroker. I didn't want to work inside. I did not want to wear a suit. I was afraid of the suit. I was clear about that. Now I just had to get clear about what I did want to do and how I could make it pay.

I was land rich and cash poor. I'd soon struggle to make the monthly payments on my properties, so I moved to sell them quickly. I knew the worry of making payments today wasn't worth the possibility the equity might increase in the future. I reduced the prices on everything I owned to twenty percent below what the last sales showed they were worth, and I offered a six percent sales commission to the broker. It was a drastic sacrifice. I lost maybe half a million dollars' worth of real estate overnight—but it worked. I sold everything in a couple of weeks, I didn't go bankrupt, and I had a few thousand dollars left in the bank. I was sad but satisfied.

Then I went to my dad.

"Dad, you know that big roll I was on in real estate?"

"Yes." That was all he said, waiting to hear what I would say next.

"Well, it's gone now, and so are all my properties. I didn't want to worry about the monthly payments, and I didn't want to declare bankruptcy. So I sold them."

I sighed. It was a deep sigh—so deep it surprised me, tinged as it was with both sadness and relief. After ten years in real estate, ten excellent years that allowed me to spend half my time traveling to find some of the best waves on the planet, I realized how good I had it and how much I was loving life. Just then, I could sense a deep void. Only at that very minute did I grasp the full impact of the stress my financial predicament had presented. Only then did I become aware of the enormous relief I felt knowing I had resolved it.

"That sounds like a smart move you made, son."

And he waited, again, for what I would say next. That was my dad.

"I don't know what I want to do now," I said.

Of course, I thought about my dad's advice ten years earlier when I returned from Stanford and didn't know what I should do for a job.

You can be a sanitation worker, you can be a waiter, you can work construction. The advice from a decade earlier dropped in as if I had just heard it yesterday. *Just learn to do the best in the business you're in. And pretty soon, you might find yourself not so excited about it anyway, and you'll want to move on. So move on.*

"And..." I paused. "Well, I just don't feel like working right now."

I was a little chagrined to have to admit that. I was thirty-two years old. What thirty-two-year-old man admits that out loud to his dad?

"I can certainly understand that." He sat back in his chair and raised his eyebrows in wait.

I took a breath. My next question tumbled out of my mouth almost all at once.

"May I live in your Puamana condo in Lahaina Town for a year? Just for a year, and I'll pay you the rent after a year?" I asked quickly. "I don't want to have a rental payment. Can... would you do something like that for me until I can figure out where I'm going?"

When Dad looked up, his face took on an odd but pleasant calm that I find hard to describe. Perhaps my vulnerability triggered something in him, as if I were not a grown man talking with him like equals in his living room, but like the boy he had guided through life to this very day. Maybe because he was missing Jimbo, he was deeply, poignantly aware of the fragility of every single thing and the preciousness of a single moment. I have no idea what was going on in his mind. But this I believe to be true: it was as if, at that moment, my dad chose to move to wonder instead of judgment. I could just feel it. It wouldn't have surprised me if he had reached out to hold my hand as he would sometimes when I was little. It was a beautiful moment—a surreal instance—and I knew, of course, it wouldn't last.

So I dumped the big one on him.

"I might become a professional windsurfer."

Innovation Incubator

I was at a party one night with Mike and another friend, Bill King, who was friends with my younger brother, Bill. It was 1981. I asked them if they wanted to open a windsurfing shop. I had a few thousand dollars left from unloading all my properties, and I figured this would be a decent investment.

We were windsurfing Ho'okipa regularly, and we were getting good. We were pushing our limits—and beyond. Mike would swipe my boards because he was always breaking his, and our masts didn't hold up for long in the winds at Ho'okipa. That slowed us down because new masts had to come on a boat from Oahu. Boards were made on the island, but they took a whole day to shape, and they weren't cheap.

The three of us were essentially pioneering the sport, pushing ourselves and trying new tricks, which meant we were breaking a lot of equipment. We would rig 'em and bust 'em. Then we started adding features to our sailboards, which meant we needed even more boards to experiment with. One day I put a mast on my shortest surfboard—it was just six and a half feet, maybe—and I took it out. The wind was blowing thirty to forty knots. I couldn't believe how sweetly that little board performed.

We were onto something. We needed to have equipment on hand. We needed an inventory in our own backyard.

Mike was winning world championships—he was maybe one of the top ten windsurfers in the world in the early 1980s. There was no money to be made from championships or sponsors—yet—but Mike was making a name for himself, thanks to the play he got in publications like *Windsurfing International*.

Mike and Bill—we call him BK—took about a split second to jump on the idea of opening a windsurfing shop. We called it Sailboards Maui.

I moved out of the house in Kahului, where I had lived with Jimbo. We cleaned out the garage—which was no small task after thirty years of Haywood family living—and that's where we started Sailboards Maui, producing and selling cutting-edge windsurfing equipment built for speed and tricks on the water.

We certainly didn't realize it at the time, but that shop in a three-bedroom house with a three-car garage near the Kahului harbor would become ground zero for windsurfing in the 1980s, accelerating the popularity of the sport around the world at hyperspeed.

I think I put in six grand and BK put up the same. We didn't ask Mike for money. He brought his reputation as the world champion. John Severson, the artist, filmmaker, and founder of *Surfer* magazine, designed our logo. I wasn't all that interested in the business itself. I was hoping that our company would be successful, or my ability to sail better would catapult me into something that might make money. I didn't know. All Mike and I wanted to do was surf—we were terrible businessmen. Thank goodness we had BK. He was the only one with any business sense. If it weren't for him, Sailboards Maui never would have made a dime.

Mike was a master at getting his board to fly across the waves, doing awesome photo-worthy tricks to impress and showcase his advertising clients. I was discovering my knack for speed. We both were pushing the limits of high-performance wave sailing.

We started using shortboards, which lent themselves to high speed, fancy tricks, sailing in the waves, and jumping. A shortboard—just over six feet—skims the surface of the water, and the speed increases when you turn. The nimbler shortboard dramatically improved our ability to move through the waves.

We were taking the sport of windsurfing to the leading edge and innovating the heck out of it.

For example, we invented the water start. Typically, you'd stand on a longboard with the sail lying in the water. You'd grab the rope to pull up the sail, and the wind would take it from there. A shortboard doesn't provide enough buoyancy to start while standing on it—it'll sink if you aren't moving. We found a way to lie on the board and push the sail up until the wind could catch it. Then we would let the sail pull us up, instead of the other way around like in a standard start. We called it the water start.

Mike was the first to do it in a course race, and I wrote the first article about how to do a water start for *Windsurf* magazine. Now everyone does it. You have to water start if you want to sail a shortboard.

Not only were we devising new windsurfing techniques, but conventional manufacturers' equipment became obsolete. It just couldn't meet our demands. We needed a shaper who could turn our requests into a finely tuned and responsive piece of fiberglass that would take our direction and magically skim the water. We convinced Jimmy Lewis, who had made his first windsurfing board for Mike a couple of years earlier, to build our custom boards. He built a shaping room in his house in Kihei, but his landlord made him tear it out. So Jimmy brought all that lumber to the Kahului house and built his shop there.

Bringing on Jimmy to shape boards for Sailboards Maui was a game-changer. He built us boards that met our demands, anticipated our needs, and satisfied even our smallest requests. Jimmy added patches where the foot straps were. He put inserts into plugs to drill the screws into the board. He was putting inserts inside the board and padding them.

Today, Jimmy Lewis is a celebrity in the windsurfing world. His boards have broken countless speed records. His boards are in such demand that he's scaled his business. They are built in a Vietnamese factory, still made by hand, just the way he makes them himself.

One day in 1982, Jimmy was shaping a board when he slipped with the block planer, putting a little gouge in the foam on the bottom. So he shaped that gouge into a teardrop-shaped concave dip in the low part of the rocker, the wide point of the board, and put it on the rack to sell. A Frenchman named Pascal Maka came to Sailboards Maui soon after and bought that eight-foot six-inch wave board. He took it to the speed trials in Weymouth, England, where he rode it to 27.8 knots and broke the world windsurfing record. That got our little Maui windsurfing shop a lot of attention, and we took advantage of it.

The next time Pascal came into our shop, he pulled a page from a magazine out of his pocket. It was an ad for Sailboards Maui, and it had a picture of him making a turn at the end of the speed run on that board Jimmy made for him. The caption read "Sailboards Maui: World's Fastest Boards."

Pascal wanted us to pay him for using his picture in our ad. I just laughed.

"Look, Pascal, we operate on a shoestring," I said. "We're just having fun here. You want money? I can't do that. But maybe I can give you a discount on another board if you want."

I think I might have sold him another of Jimmy's boards at half price, which was our cost.

"And you know what?" I added. "I'll just come over to England next year and kick your butt."

And I did.

The next year I won Weymouth. And I won it with a sail my buddy Barry Spanier made.

Barry was making sails for boats in Lahaina, and his sails were sold all over the world. Mike asked him to make a custom sail for a windsurfer. That's when we started using Maui Sails.

The next year, I asked Barry to make me a sail to take to Weymouth. I wanted to beat Pascal's world record. Barry outfitted me with a great TriRadial wave sail. But it was the innovative wing mast he developed with Dimitri Milovic that gave me a split-second advantage. The mast was shaped like a teardrop instead of round. The inner skin was foam, and the outer skin was carbon fiber and cooked in an oven. The sail ran up a track in the back, rather than wrapping around it. I could adjust the curve by turning the wing and holding it in place. When there was less wind, I wanted more foil, more curve in the sail. When the winds got stronger, I wanted a flatter sail. I could do this with the wing mast. The wing mast was superior simply because it was more efficient. The aerodynamics were perfect, and I could feel the acceleration it gave me.

We were inventing and improving the gear for the short-board era, an evolution in windsurfing we were perfecting. I called it "R & D"... Rip-off and Development. We would see what our competitors were doing, then make it better. We just copied and improved on the existing equipment. We were an incubator of sorts. We would pay people to make what we needed to our specifications. Then they'd go out and launch successful businesses.

For example, Mike went to a small shop on Maui that made surfboard leashes. It was the only place with a sewing machine that could sew through Velcro, webbing, and thick fabrics like wetsuit material, and it had only been in business a couple of years. He asked the owner, Rob Kaplan, if he could make foot straps to meet our specifications. Rob could, he did, and he met our requests time and again. Rob started Dakine Hawaii in 1979—and he sold it in 2009 for a hundred million dollars.

Lenny Cappe worked for us for six months and then left to open Hawaiian Island Windsurfing. We hired Paul Ehman to run our events, and he later became an event producer and made a ton of money. We worked with Barry Spanier and Geoffrey Bourne to make windsurfing sails. And, of course, Jimmy Lewis eventually went out on his own, and he's still making the best boards on the planet.

We taught these guys how to make a business, and they'd figure out how to make it profitable. Sadly, that was something we never figured out ourselves! We spent too much time on the water and too little time in the business. Essentially, we trained them and showed them what not to do—don't go windsurfing every day.

Nevertheless, Mike and I left BK in the shop to run the business while we went in search of success for Sailboards Maui—and ourselves—on the water.

The Maui Grand Prix

I t's a bold claim: In 1981, Sailboards Maui opened, putting the island of Maui on the map and making it the windsurfing capital of the world in just a year or two. The island provided the perfect angle of trade winds for the consistent surf on the north shore. Jimmy was building a board a day, and that wasn't fast enough for the demand. Mike Waltze's championship status turned the surfing world's attention our way, and I was winning a few contests myself.

Those were the evolutionary days of windsurfing, attracting devotees from around the world to our island and the charming little town of Paia, just a few miles from Ho'okipa Beach. In the early twentieth century, Paia was home to the plantation workers of the Paia Sugar Mill before they moved to Dream City in Kahului to own their homes. About the time we showed up, Paia was home to hippies, thanks to its affordable rents and the nearby beaches. It was little more than a ghost town compared to the hustle it boasts today. You could park just about anywhere on the street in 1980. Buildings painted in sixties-era pastels, reminiscent of a California beach town with a Wild West accent, housed fish stores and small mom-and-pop stores catering to the locals....

Until we held the first Maui Grand Prix in 1981.

At the time, Kailua on Oahu was the epicenter for the sport, and the Pan Am Cup was the premier windsurfing event in the world. In 1980, Mike and I flew over to compete, only to find the winds were blowing under thirteen knots. No one could sail, so they canceled the race. We called BK to find out if there was wind on Maui. There was. We sure weren't going to sit around and miss a day on the water, so Mike and I jumped on an airplane and flew home. Back in those days, Hawaiian Airlines and Aloha Airlines sold books of tickets between Kahului and Honolulu for twenty-five bucks a flight. It was like buying a bus ticket.

We enjoyed a great afternoon on the water. When the winds slowed at the end of the day, we packed up our gear and headed right back to the airport. We flew back to Oahu and told everybody at the contest that, while they were just sitting around drinking beers, we had sailed mast-high waves in twenty-five-knot winds at Ho'okipa.

Mike, BK, and I decided to organize the first wave contest at Ho'okipa. We called the event the Expression Session, and it previewed what Maui had to offer windsurfers. We drew a decent crowd, drumming them up by passing the word. In those days, before the internet, that meant picking up the phone. Windsurfers in 1980 were a fairly small but zealous group, so it wasn't hard to get them to show up. They got to experience firsthand Ho'okipa's perfect wind direction and the steep waves from the deep water dropping into the shallow reef. And because the action was so close to shore, photographers could get some great shots.

Mike invited photographers he knew from his work in advertising, and they proved to the windsurfing world that Maui just might be its epicenter. The publicity we generated from that little exhibition contest opened the floodgates for the Maui Grand

Prix, a wave sailing event that became one of the most prestigious high-performance windsurfing competitions in the world.

None of us at Sailboards Maui had put on any sort of contest before. The Expression Session was our first, a sort of beta test, and it turned out to be a successful one. We decided we could do another, bigger one and maybe make some money at it.

The next summer, in 1981, Sailboards Maui sponsored the Maui Grand Prix—the first of what would be three annual competitions attracting windsurfers and spectators from around the world. It later morphed into the Aloha Classic.

We got lucky that first year. Major League Baseball went on strike, canceling a third of the schedule in the middle of the season. Mike, because he was so hooked in to the press channels, learned television networks were looking for an event. We offered them a great one! Maui was crawling with media, all come to fill their sports programs and pages with a watersport most people had never seen. And, it seemed, they couldn't get enough of windsurfing after that first televised contest.

The second year, the whole world was following us. Windsurfers came from Japan, Australia, and all over North America. We even had guys come from England, Switzerland, and Africa. We drummed up eight thousand dollars in prizes from sponsors. Mike Waltze and Robbie Naish, who was eighteen and had been windsurfing for five years, were the big names. Julie DeWerd from Honolulu was one of five women who competed. She was just twenty-three and had only been windsurfing for a year. The girls competed with the guys, and they did a great job holding their own. At thirty-two years old, I was the oldest. A journalist covering the event called me the "oldest living big wave windsurfer." I don't know if that's something I should be proud of or not. I just know I did not win anything—Matt Schweitzer and Klaus Simmer both beat me.

The competition featured three events: course racing, dual surf slalom, and an event we premiered, the world's first freestyle, now called wave riding, which involved wave surfing and jumping.

The freestyle took place last. Baron Arnaud de Rosnay was another of the notables attending the Maui Grand Prix in '82. Arnaud was perhaps the most famous windsurfer at the time for his cross-country and distance records. He had a particular lack of respect for the freestyle—he preferred speed.

The son of a French aristocrat, Arnaud was a fashion photographer who shot for *Vogue* and other international magazines, and he came to Maui to shoot the Maui Grand Prix competition. He had lived in India with the Beatles. He hung with the Rolling Stones. He was married to windsurfer Jenna Severson, daughter of *Surfer* magazine founder John Severson, who designed the Sailboards Maui logo.

He and Mike had a love-hate relationship with each other when it came to windsurfing. Mike loved to do tricks on the waves, while Arnaud thrived on speed.

"Oh, you are like a clown who dances out in the waves and does silly things," Arnaud said to Mike once. "But I am a speed sailor, and I go through channels to other countries, and this is more magnificent."

Mike and his childhood buddy Matt Schweitzer competed in the final freestyle event. Julie had given it her best shot but was eliminated early in the finals. The event had a twenty-point system: you could earn five points for jumping, five points for style, and ten points for riding the waves. Judges sat casually at a picnic table on the beach, which was packed with photographers and spectators gathered on Ho'okipa's rocky shoreline to watch the sailors perform.

"They need just to not get caught by a big wave," Arnaud said in an interview before the jumping competition. "These competitors are the best in the world. They want to be able to jive very fast, to be very maneuverable. You'll see the best guys able to stand up among the others."

He was right, of course. The judges looked for the guy who offered the most sensational demonstration of dancing the waves—the most turning, catching the most waves and performing the most radical maneuvers. The guy to win the world's first freestyle wave surfing and jumping event turned out to be Mike Waltze.

"I just tried to do as many turns as I could to impress the judges," Mike said after the race. "And try not to fall."

Robby Naish won the Maui Windsurfing Grand Prix 1982 overall title.

The Maui Grand Prix accelerated an explosion in the sport at just the right time. Magazines were writing about us. Sailing stars and casual windsurfers were coming from the West Coast and from all over the world. They were coming to Sailboards Maui specifically.

Competitive windsurfing would never be the same. And neither would Maui.

Endorphins

Windsurfing contests like the Maui Grand Prix were far from antagonistic competitions. Those of us who were developing expanding this new sport relished the opportunity to get together, show off our latest maneuvers, and collaborate.

The same was true of running Sailboards Maui. Sure, the shop was a business, and we had to take that seriously. But I never was so pumped as when I was hanging out with BK, Jimmy, and Mike every single day—much of it on the water.

I have a personal theory—something I made up—that when you produce endorphins together, you share them, too. Endorphins are "feel-good" chemicals the body makes that produce a sense of euphoria and bliss. Exercise boosts the production, which is why they are attributed to a "runner's high." When my buddies and I enjoyed a high together, when we shared a rush on the water, we intermingled those feel-good chemicals.

Nothing cements camaraderie like being blown away on the water with your friends. I learned this when I was swimming at Santa Clara, I experienced it again with Gerry Lopez in Bali, and I found it to be just as true with these guys. Life was good.

Jimmy and I lived together in a house at Kuau Point, the closest we could get to Ho'okipa Beach, about a mile east of Paia and next door to Mama's Fish House. Mama's is now a treasured Maui institution popular with tourists and requiring reservations. But back then, it was a small neighborhood restaurant frequented by the locals for the fresh fish caught by Maui fishermen. Each day, the restaurant would print the names of the fishermen and where the fish was caught on the menu.

Jimmy and I loved living at Kuau because we could launch our sailboards right off the point. I kept half a dozen of Jimmy's custom speed boards all rigged up and ready to go. I just had to perch one on my head, walk down the rocks, step out into our little channel, and get out into the surf. I would sail early in the morning and later in the day until the last wind on the island was just enough to get me home.

Friends would sometimes sail downwind with me. They loved the exhilaration of the speed bursts, especially behind some breaking waves, while sailing across the smooth foam layer, the speeds would increase.

It was more intense during the winter—huge swells intensified the challenge. Many times I had to do a perfect jibe to avoid and outrun a giant breaking wave in my path. I experienced some big crashes which ended in a paddle in to the beach. It was all pretty safe, as the waves washed in toward the shore, and onshore crosswinds would push me along.

Sometimes I would sail at full speed down to Kanaha Beach near the airport by myself. The run—maybe seven miles—would take me fifteen or twenty minutes. I was unable to sail back upwind on those tiny speed needles, so I would take apart my equipment, walk out of Kanaha Beach Park and wait for another windsurfer driving to Ho'okipa to pick me up. I did this two or three times a day.

Back then, even with a surfboard, hitchhiking on Maui was common transportation. People driving past began to recognize me and would pull over. When I got back home or to Ho'okipa, I'd jumped in the water and do it again. Then I'd jump in the water and do it again until I knew that I could sail off the wind very fast.

I started windsurfing eight miles across the Pailolo Channel to the island of Molokai with Bill Boyum, Mike Waltze, Matt Schweitzer, and anyone else who wanted to go. Mike, Matt, and I were sailing to Molokai one day. We were sitting on our boards just out of sight of the island when Arnaud De Rosnay came sailing up to us.

"Mike, Fred, Matt, follow me!" Arnaud called to us in his French accent. "I will show you the way to the beach!"

The three of us looked at each other a little quizzically. Then, we almost fell off our boards laughing.

We sailed over to Molokai a lot. We knew the channels and where to go. We certainly knew where the beach was. It was just like Arnaud, with his charisma tinged with a touch of aristocracy, to act like he knew more about windsurfing, even around the Hawaiian Islands.

Arnaud had earned the right to lead us to the Molokai beach, and anywhere else, for that matter. Breaking windsurfing records for several years, Arnaud fancied himself a sort of peace pilgrim with an ambitious, albeit impossible, goal to bring hostile countries together by sailing the straits that separated them.

In 1979, he sailed the Bering Strait between Alaska and Siberia. His sail displayed the American flag on the bottom half and the Soviets' on top, symbolizing the unity he hoped to forge by bridging the two countries. On that adventure, the only cultural sharing turned out to be of champagne, caviar, and plenty of toasts between Arnaud and Soviet officials. He always was a charmer.

Arnaud attempted, unsuccessfully, to cross the English Channel. He later sailed from Miami to Cuba. He followed that up with crossing the Strait of La Perouse between Japan and the Soviet Union.

Shortly after I met him, he attempted the impossible, sailing between Tahiti and Hawaii. On that crossing, he disappeared for eleven days until the French Navy found him on an island called Ahé in French Polynesia. A local found him marooned on the beach.

The French government tried to stop him from sailing to Hawaii. But he wanted the fame and the glory—that was just Arnaud's personality. So he was going for it. One night he took off by himself, and sailing downwind, headed west. He carried a photovoltaic water purifier on his sailboard. He took a kite he could use to pull him. He also had pontoons he would blow up so he could sleep on the board and stay drier.

I saw him when he got back to Maui. His face was blistered from the sun. His arms were rubbed raw from holding onto the board. His knees were pretty scraped up too, probably from using the kite when he couldn't stand and hold the sail. He told me he fended off sharks with a Swiss Army knife, poking them in the nose if they came too close.

"Arnaud," I told him when I saw him, "you get so lucky on these crazy adventures. I gave you just a fifty percent chance of making it on this one.

"Oh, no," he said. "I've got it together. You know I can handle it."

So he started planning a new adventure to sail the Formosa Strait from China to Taiwan. It would prove to be his last.

After Arnaud left for China with all his gear, he discovered his mast broke. On a layover in Hong Kong, he picked up a two-piece mast. It wasn't an ideal replacement for the challenging crossing, which, sadly, is stating the obvious now. Arnaud set off for what should have been an eight-hour crossing, but he disappeared, and a ten-day search by air and sea found no trace of a board, a sail, or a body. Plenty of supposition surrounds his disappearance—and even more rumors—but all I know is that no one heard from him again.

The day Arnaud found us just shy of the Molokai shore, we were happy to see him. With no idea that it would be one of the last opportunities we would have to sail together, we took him up on his offer to be our tour guide. We all liked Arnaud and enjoyed his company, bluster and all. We popped up onto our boards and let him lead us straight in to the beach.

We would sail to Molokai once a week or more during the summer when the afternoon high tides made it manageable to sail over the shallow reefs.

One day Matt Schweitzer went with us—without his harness! A harness wraps around your waist and hooks to the boom of the sail. It takes the weight of the sail off your arms so that you can sail more efficiently, especially over long distances and in open waters.

We were hanging out one rainy day at Matt's house, which was on the west side of Maui near Napili. There wasn't enough wind to do much, but Matt decided to take his board out to do freestyle tricks in the light air.

All of a sudden, the winds picked up, and whitecaps were everywhere. The rest of us jumped on our boards and sailed out to meet Matt. Someone suggested we head to Molokai, and off we went.

Matt made the trip over, but just barely.

"Man," he said when he caught up to us, "I'm so tired. I forgot my harness! I came all that way without it!"

He had held that grueling pressure with his arms for twenty minutes, and then he had to make the return trip home.

I had an equipment catastrophe myself late one afternoon when Peter Boyd and I sailed over to Molokai. It was about five in the afternoon, and we were halfway back to Maui when my mast broke in half. I couldn't see the beaches on any coastline—Maui, Molokai, or Lanai. That's how far out we were.

There I sat on my board with the mast in pieces in my lap and my board slightly underwater. Seawater swashed all around me and my gear. I always carried a roll of duct tape, and I was fiddling with everything.

Peter sat on his rig, watching me try to devise a way to cobble together the pieces to sail back to Molokai. I knew Mike had stowed a spare mast somewhere, just in case. Equipment breaks all the time, and this was the time for it. I just had no idea where to find it.

"Fred!" Peter called suddenly, and I heard a hint of panic in his voice.

I looked up to see him staring over my shoulder at the water behind me.

"I think I see a shark!"

For a minute, my heart stopped. But just for a minute. I glared at him. I spoke slowly and calmly.

"Peter. If you thought you saw a shark, you didn't. I'm not going to freak out and drop all this gear in the water. I'll never be able to do anything then. If you thought you saw a shark, you didn't see a shark. Shut up.

"By the way, Peter," I added. "You're the one carrying raw venison on your back."

He had frozen venison in his backpack from Molokai. That shut him up. I went back to my repair.

At that time, windsurfing components were in pieces. I rolled up the sail and tucked it under one leg along with the two parts of the broken mast. My base had a two-piece extension. One piece had a collar on it that slid up to adjust the length of the sail as needed. I took that piece and slid it inside the broken mast pieces. It fit well enough. With my emergency repair kit—duct tape!—I taped the parts together well enough to get me back to Molokai. I inched my way back with Peter. The sail was so loose it waved like a flag behind the mast.

We got there at about eight o'clock that night, and I called Mike.

"Mike," I said, "you left a mast on Molokai yesterday, didn't you? I broke my mast on the way back to Maui. I need it to get home. You hid it in the bushes somewhere. Where the hell is it?"

He told me where along the shoreline he had hidden it. It was dark, so we knew we weren't going anywhere till the next day, and we made plans to sleep on the beach. The next day we found the mast. That's how I made it back to Maui the following day.

I made that trip to Molokai at least once a month, and I probably did it fifty times. Each morning when I got up, I would check the wind direction and strength. (I still do, only now there's an app for that!) One day, Bill Boyum and I decided it had been way too long since our last channel run to Molokai, and we needed a fix. We loaded up our gear on top of my car and headed around the northwest side of Maui to Arnaud's house in Napili to see if he wanted to go with us. But the wind was too light and at a wrong angle for a fast run to Molokai.

Frustrated, we drove back toward Kahului. As we approached Wahikuli Beach, just before Lahaina, we pulled over to scope out a solid line of big whitecaps that had popped up. They headed south past Lahaina and filled in solidly to the island of Lanai. It was a freak wind with a freak swell. We had never sailed to Lanai before, and suddenly the way there was laid out before us like a magic carpet. We were ready.

Such favorable conditions can quickly change, so we just set up and went. We had no water or food with us because we knew Arnaud would have loaded us with supplies had we spent the day with him. We didn't let that stop us from what looked like an incredible sail to Lanai.

The run was even more spectacular than we could have imagined. Because the early morning sun was behind us, the water sparkled like it had small diamonds dotting the surface. The wind, at maybe thirty miles an hour, was intense, of course, but the added element of a large north swell running through the channel created huge mountains with smooth faces in the ocean. We could bear off them, like dropping in on a huge wave. The waves were perfectly aligned. We could stay on a wave for hundreds of yards, then go to the next one, and the next one.

It's seven miles as the crow flies from Lahaina to Lanai. We did practically fly there, indeed, averaging more than twenty miles an hour and making Shipwreck Beach in twenty minutes.

Lanai is aerodynamically shaped, and the wind blows strong along the east coast. Bill and I reached Lanai's shore and moved inside the shallow reef, running a good eight miles along the coast facing Maui at full speed over smooth, glassy water just deep enough to clear our fins. We knew to take care. You can't swim there—the rough waters make it too dangerous. Strong north winds between the islands create a venturi effect, resulting in powerful currents that have forced ships onto the hazardous reefs; hence, the name "Shipwreck Beach."

The day was getting on, and we knew from our many sails to Molokai that the wind could lighten. Around four-thirty in the afternoon, the land would heat up, and the winds would lighten. We turned to head back to Maui. Sure enough, the wind steadily decreased. We got a mile offshore from Lahaina, and we couldn't sail any further. We took our sails apart, rolled our masts up inside the sails, laid all the gear between our bodies and our boards, and awkwardly paddled to shore.

By the time we reached land, we had been sailing for four or five hours without food or water. My underarms were raw from rubbing the sandpaper-like textured deck of my board, while I paddled a mile. We were so hungry that we each bought a bag of Famous Amos chocolate chip cookies, poured a quart of milk in the bag, shook it up, and scarfed down cookies in milk.

Bill said that sail to Lanai was the most magnificent, memorable run he ever experienced windsurfing, better than any he's had sailing at Ho'okipa. He said it even topped hang gliding. It was a remarkable day because we were spontaneous. We saw the excellent conditions and said, "Wow! Look at it. It's good! Let's go!" If we had stopped to find food and water to take with us, the opportunity would have passed.

Adventures like that one have connected me with my friends for life. The greater the stoke, the stronger the friendships. No matter how competitive we might have been, we still respected each other because we trained together, we swam together, we windsurfed together. We were abused physically together in training. We experienced similar pressures of competition in the pool and the challenges of wave riding.

Now we have a perpetual camaraderie. There's not a time I can't meet these friends and have hugs and love—no matter how long it's been since we've seen each other—because we shared endorphins.

If my theory is correct, Laird Hamilton and I will always be "blood brothers," as he calls us.

Laird has been surfing since he was a kid. But he didn't start windsurfing until he discovered shortboards. He has said he wasn't interested in the sport until he could put a sail on a shortboard. So I guess Sailboards Maui can count this awesome waterman as one of our "innovations," getting him off the surfboard, behind a sail, and eventually to Maui, just as the action was starting.

But to get Laird to move to Maui, I had to run with him on what was perhaps the most endorphin-generating experience of my life.

I went over to Kauai for a couple of weeks to sail with Laird in 1984. I saw his raw talent. One day we were sailing Tunnels Beach on the north shore near Hanalei, which may be the most beautiful beach in Hawaii. Towering over it is the mystical, pyramid-shaped Makana Mountain, popularly known as Bali Hai from *South Pacific*. The Tunnels surf break is one of the most challenging. I discovered that for myself the day we were there.

Laird and I spent the morning sailing six- to ten-foot waves. After lunch, we returned to find the wind had picked up, and the beach was empty. The winds were westerly, flying at forty to fifty miles an hour, maybe stronger. Our boards and sails, which we had firmly planted in the sand before we left, drifted closer to the ocean with each gust of wind.

"Let's do a coast run," Laird said.

These days, Laird is known for his willingness to confront fear head-on. He claims fear makes you see better, it makes you hear better, it makes you think better— once you're used to harnessing it. That day he proved it to me.

I looked at the sea and could find no exit. It was a complete whiteout. I confronted Laird's courage and harnessed every bit of my own to match it.

"Okay," I said. "Let's go. Where are we going?"

"Let's go down to Hanalei Bay."

I was on a 5.2-square-meter sail, and his was a 5.6. With the winds topping forty knots, we probably should have used sails smaller than fives. Never mind. We grabbed our gear and headed to Hanalei, about five miles east along the coast.

We had to hurdle fifteen-foot whitewater waves coming straight at us. I reared up my board right before I hit each wave. Then I sheeted in, trying to fumble over it going the opposite direction. It's a tricky maneuver, and pretty wild—impossible on a surfboard, but not with a windsurfer. A kite could also make a bit of an adjustment and carry you right over the wave, but kitesurfing wasn't around yet.

Pretty quickly, a few tumbles in the whitewater separated me from Laird. You sail with another for safety, especially in rough conditions like we had that day. If you lose sight of your partner, it's nerve-wracking.

Shortly after we took off, we passed a restaurant overlooking the water called Charos. Everyone in the restaurant had come to the windows to watch us try to break through. Eventually, I made it over one final huge whitewater to open water, and there was Laird.

Off we headed to Hanalei Bay.

We found each other about a mile or two out from the coast. The wind was still blowing at forty to fifty miles per hour. The waves were twenty to thirty feet, and coming from the north was a twenty-foot swell, creating a lot of crisscrossing waves.

The wind was almost overpowering. It was an incredible challenge to power through the massive twenty-foot waves crashing on the reefs with fifty-knot winds generating thirty-foot running seas outside. We sailed at a beam reach—ninety degrees—to the wind direction on the coast run. It was risky. We had to avoid the towering swells and breaking crests everywhere, plus we had to turn further downwind—ninety to a hundred and thirty-five degrees—which increases speeds and risk tremendously.

I figured out that once I was speeding down a running swell, I could sheet in all the way, closing my sail parallel and over my board, and turn a hundred and eighty degrees downwind using the gravity and speed generated to ride effortlessly down the massive slope to the trough, much like surfing the wave. Then I'd slow down and hold position to wait for the same wave to catch up, lifting me to the crest where the wind is strongest. At this that point, I would immediately sheet out, opening my sail to ninety degrees, and turn my board perpendicular to the wind again while luffing my sail (completely de-powering it) to handle the massive gusts. I would adjust my sail and repeat the same moves with every passing swell.

I had never sailed like that before. It required an immense amount of concentration.

I looked over to Laird to see him jumping thirty feet in the air and landing flat on his board next to me. He was asking for disaster.

Laird has always been a daredevil on the water. *Surfer* magazine called him "surfing's biggest, boldest, bravest, and the best big-wave surfer in the world today, bar none."

While I might not have had his unflinching courage, I had around fifteen years on him, a lot more experience, and apparently a lot more common sense.

"Laird!" I hollered at him. "STOP! Stop jumping! You can lose everything!"

The currents underwater were running at five knots, with the winds blowing at around fifty. That certainly was not the day to be doing tricks on the waves. If either of us broke down, we wouldn't be able to find the other because the waves were too high.

Laird and I ran the rest of the run together. We reached Hanalei and turned into the bay with the wind behind us. That made it tough to reach the side shores, and we had to work to maneuver the breaks. When we got into the bay, we found the windsurfers there on four-meter sails—much smaller than ours, and more appropriate for the high winds.

We also found Laird's younger brother, Lyon. Lyon was freaking out. He had been with us at Tunnels that morning but left at midday for lunch. When he came back to find us, we were gone. Even our boards were missing. But Laird's car was still at the beach. The conditions were such that it never occurred to him that we might do a coast run. When he saw us flying with the winds into the bay, through the massive whitewater, he and everyone watching on the beach were astounded—and pretty impressed.

We went sailing the next morning, and the winds were still strong. Laird attempted his first jump and broke the fin off his board when he hit the water. All I could think was how fortunate we were that he didn't break his fin the day before. I just had a sense that he was pushing it too much, and I was glad I stopped him.

Reflecting on that coast run from Tunnels to Hanalei, I recall it was that day Laird said we became "blood brothers." To this day, either of us can call the other and we pick right up where we left off, no matter how long since we last spoke. I, of course, attribute our three-plus decades of friendship to the stoke we shared that day.

It was only the first of many adventures Laird and I would share. It wasn't long before Laird moved to Maui. I convinced him that he needed to put himself in the middle of all the innovations and the competition we were attracting and the photographers who were looking to shoot the insane tricks Laird was so very good at.

Weymouth

thought I might have been kidding both of us the day I told my dad I might become a professional windsurfer. And then I did.

The most notable contest in the early years of speed sailing was in England. Weymouth Speed Week was the first speed sailing event in the world. It runs each year in Portland Harbour on the English Channel coast. The harbor is ideally suited for its smooth, strong winds and flat water, especially in the fall. For years, Weymouth showcased sailboats reaching world record-breaking speeds and demonstrating advancements in technologies. Windsurfing was a recent addition to the competition, and it already had a reputation for being a big event where records were broken.

The year before, Pascal Maka set a world record at 27.8 knots on Jimmy Lewis's custom board—the one he picked up at Sailboards Maui with the prototype concave teardrop carved into it to compensate for Jimmy's accidental nick. We called it an innovation by accident because that concave shape in the bottom turned out to be a speed accelerator. (Pascal later came back and asked for some money because we used his picture in a Sailboards Maui advertisement.) I had a personal, albeit friendly, competitive urge to beat Pascal in the competition.

I asked Barry Spanier if he would support my intention to set a world record at Weymouth, and he was all in. He agreed to make sails for the wing mast Dimitri Milovic designed—that aerodynamic mast with a teardrop shape, much like an airplane wing, that would decrease wind resistance.

In October 1983, Barry Spanier and I headed to Europe for the speed competition—my first professional contest. I'd only windsurfed competitively on Maui before, so I was pretty stoked about this trip.

I flew to France, where I sailed—miserably—in a contest in Brest. There were three hundred fifteen entrants in the Brest Speed Week. My biggest board was a custom eight and a half foot Jimmy Lewis board with a concave bottom running into a soft "V" in the tail. I was using Barry's wing mast and booms, but I opted for a small sail, anticipating big winds. I anticipated wrong and found myself on the water with a sinking board and a mast that was too heavy for the wind—or lack of it. The winds may not have exceeded eighteen knots all week, and I could not start my tiny board, for the winds were just too light.

I finished 315th—last place.

I knew I had to turn things around for Weymouth. I came with great equipment, so I did not feel defeated. I was determined that failure would not find me.

My buddy from Maui, Klaus Simmer, was competing in Brest, too. He handed down his rig to me after France was over and before I ventured off to the next speed contest across the channel. When I got to Weymouth, the race organizers assigned me the number thirteen and gave me the stickers for my sail. I didn't mind—since my disappointment the week before in Brest, how could I do any worse than last place?

Barry headed directly to Weymouth about ten days before the contest with a supply of wing masts and sail material. He brought his wife and son along. Dimitri showed up in a Volkswagen with a load of wing masts strapped to the roof. We didn't know for sure that these masts would work. The few I had tested on Maui failed. But I had a good feeling about them anyway.

Barry and Dimitri found a local sail loft where they could work. They were my support team. We all stayed in a small house we rented for seventy-five pounds. We had no money, so Barry's wife, Theresa, would take some cash to the local shops and bring home pasta, or whatever was cheap, to cook.

When I got to England a few days before the competition, the weather wasn't cooperating any more than it had in France. We spent our time tuning my equipment and heading to the beach to check the conditions. There we were at the Weymouth Speed Trials, famous for powerful winds, smooth waters, and ideal wind-surfing conditions, and there was no wind.

Until Wednesday.

On Tuesday, the weather reports predicted a low-pressure zone—a "Black Wednesday." I knew my luck had changed, and the weather would be perfect for my board, the carbon wing mast, and my sail emblazoned with the number thirteen.

We got up Wednesday morning, and it was as if all hell had broken loose. All of a sudden, the winds had picked up, going from twenty knots the day before to fifty. A wall of black brought a storm of rain, and it was freezing. We put on our weather gear, bundled up, and headed over in the van.

You have to imagine the scene that day. All sorts of craft—not just windsurfers— were invited to participate at Weymouth. The open-class record was thirty-six knots, held by Crossbow II, a catamaran owned by Timothy Colman of Colman's Mustard. We found out later that Johnnie Walker was offering a prize of £15,000 to anyone who could best the Crossbow record. We didn't know there was a prize. That was a lot of money, especially since we came over with next to none. But we just wanted to break the record.

Large catamarans, including one powered by a Jacob's ladder, a stack of Flexifoil ten sails, small craft, and various tandem sailors and solo sailors littered the harbor, all trying to get through the same somewhat-choppy course.

We had spent the morning adjusting the rig to where it felt good. My board was an eight-foot, nine-inch round pintail with a glassed-in single fin, built much like a wave board. The wing mast attracted a lot of attention from sailors and spectators. Barry waited in a soft-sided Avon inflatable boat to pick me up and return me up to the starting line. I was watching the weather conditions. You don't want to run in light air. You don't want to run when the course is choppy or crowded with other sailors.

I stood up on the first puff and made my way to a clean speed run through the course. The wing mast proved its superiority that day! I could feel the acceleration. I could feel it jumping in my hands as if it wanted to go faster. I had never felt that from a sail until I rode the wing mast.

It was with the rising winds when the record fell, and I posted close to thirty of the fastest runs that day. On my last run, I went out and sailed a world record-breaking speed of 30.82 knots. Mission accomplished.

Call it luck; call it karma. For the second time in my life, I went from last to first in a water competition. First, it was in the Santa Clara pool racing Mitch Ivey after he taught me his backstroke. Fifteen years later, I lost at Brest, but a week later, I broke a world record and won the world speed sailing championship in Weymouth, England.

That night, we headed to the Weymouth Yacht Club, where Sir Reginald Bennet, the quartermaster of the English parliament, organized a party for us. Beer and Johnnie Walker flowed generously. Sir Reginald awarded us a gallon of whisky as a prize. Neither Barry nor I drank whisky, so we handed the bottle to our driver who said he knew just what to do with it. I guess we weren't all that surprised when he did not show up the next day.

Two days later, I prepared for another run at that prize money. Barry and I tucked my rig in a ditch at the head of the course. We sat in the van, eating our homemade lunches and waiting for wind. Suddenly, we felt the leading edge of another front blow in. Huge gusts rocked the van. They must have topped fifty knots! That's how fast the winds can change at Weymouth, and why it was the most prominent sailing contest in the early eighties. I ran down to the beach to grab my board. I had my smallest sail ready, and I got in the water to start.

The angle of the wind was perfect. I had a feeling this might be the day I could give the Crossbow a run for the record.

If ever I might think I've mastered the winds and water on a windsurfing board, Mother Nature humbles me.

Unfortunately, my start stalled, and I drifted more than a hundred yards across the starting line, losing precious seconds. Finally, a puff of wind stood me up, and I shot like a rocket through the mess of mist and rain and spray. The boom shuddered in my hands. I accelerated beyond belief and headed down the course at what I believe was the fastest run of my windsurfing career, even today. I had just completed my run when the wind blew the timer booth over, canceling the contest for the day.

I have no doubt I ran at forty knots, beating the Crossbow record. But the stopwatch recorded only thirty knots. Because of my slow start, Barry and I would go home with another bottle of Johnnie Walker and an empty wallet.

We had won the world record, but after several weeks in Weymouth, we were broke. We had to call our buddy Geoff Cornish at Neil Pryde Sails to ask for money to get home.

The Biggest Wave in the World

When I returned to Maui from Weymouth, a crowd of friends—I guess I could call them fans now—met my plane at the airport and were cheering when I exited the plane onto the tarmac.

Maui's still got a pretty small airport, but in 1983 it had only a couple of gates. The airport had just started receiving direct flights from the mainland. The parking lot had maybe forty parking spaces.

Mike Waltze had arranged for a limousine, and it was waiting for me right there on the tarmac. I climbed down the stairs from the airplane and loaded my gear into the trunk of the limo. I jumped in with Mike, Jimmy, and BK. We popped a bottle of champagne and took off for an island tour of our favorite sailing spots. It was a magnificent welcome home.

I went back to sailing every day. It was winter, and the waves were at their most extreme. I loved it because wave riding was my favorite part of the sport. After my win at Weymouth, I was even more committed to becoming a professional windsurfer. I had my eye on Neil Pryde Sails, which had given me enough money before Weymouth to cover my expenses for that trip. I planned to generate enough sponsorships to support me.

The boys and I called each other every morning to see where we were going to sail so as to have company. There were not many sailors on the island, so everywhere we sailed was never crowded.

We put on what would be our last Maui Grand Prix at Ho'okipa, and Mike Waltze won again. It was a very happy time at Sailboards Maui, and Bill King was a gem at keeping it together.

By February, winter was putting on its best show, delivering high winds and excellent waves. I had been sailing Ho'okipa for four days in a row, and the waves were growing consistently bigger every day. I had sailed six- to eight-foot waves one day, then ten- to twelve-foot waves the next. They were fifteen feet on the third day and up to twenty feet on the fourth.

On the morning of the fifth day of this incredible gift of ocean waves, Maui's north shore served up a whiteout. It was solid white-water, with the waves breaking on the outer reefs from Kahului to Ho'okipa. I was driving from Sailboards Maui east on Hana Highway to Paia when, after I passed the airport, I saw Arnaud de Rosnay driving west in a convertible Cadillac with the top down. As we approached each other, I could see him waving me down. I stopped my car right there on the road to find out what he was so fired up about.

"Fred!" Arnaud hollered. Now, Arnaud was always an enthusiastic guy, but this may have been the most wound up I had ever seen him.

"Fred! The biggest waves in the world are coming today! They are going to be at Ho'okipa! Today! Come at noon. I will have a helicopter! We will take some photographs! Show up at noon and be a part of this. It is going to be great!"

"Well, that sounds great, Arnaud. I'll come. But I'm going to be there at three-thirty."

"No! Come at twelve and get photographs! You need the publicity."

I shook my head. "Sorry, Arnaud. The biggest wave is coming at four-thirty today, and I'm going to be on it, and that's it. I'm not coming at noon. I'm only going to ride one wave. It's going to be hard to get out. You know how it is. Once you ride a wave, if you're inside, you can't get out again. That's what happens when it gets this big. I'm not going to miss that chance. It's going to be tremendous."

I went down to Ho'okipa Beach Park around three that afternoon. The helicopter was still there, hovering over the guys sailing. I could see Craig Masonville, Malte Simmer, David Ezzy, Brian Carlstom, and Mike Eskimo from the road, which is high enough to offer a great view of the water. They were all friends of mine with shops, and they were all excellent sailors. They were riding really big waves.

The road above the beach is pretty high, and as I pulled in, I watched Malte Simmer go up to face a wave, make a turn up the top, and come back down. I could barely see him making the downturn because I could see just the tops every once in a while. That wave was huge. It was the biggest thing I'd ever seen.

Once I pulled down into the parking lot and started rigging, I couldn't see anybody until they came through the break.

These really were the biggest waves I'd seen at Ho'okipa. I can't remember ever seeing bigger ones—even today, some forty years later. I rigged up a 5.9 square-meter sail on a sixteen-foot mast with a one-foot extension. I clicked into my eight-foot, nine-inch board and sailed out. It was a big rig for what I wanted to do. The winds were light, and getting through these massive whitewaters barreling into shore was the challenge. I inched out slowly around the point and caught a puff of wind to get onto a comfortable plane. The toughest part was trying to climb twenty feet of white-water mush. I got bashed by the first wave and lost my rig. I swam in to shore to retrieve my board. I took a minute to catch my breath before I sailed back out, only to wipe out again. The white-water tumbled me around like I was in a washing machine. That happened two more times.

I was expecting this. If the conditions are rough, you're not going to get through the surf to the open water easily. That's why I wanted to arrive at the beach an hour before I expected the biggest waves to hit.

Finally, I managed to maneuver through the currents to get out into the channel and face it again. I was in the clear but not moving fast. I saw a huge set off in the distance, and it seemed like only moments before the first massive wave was feathering about two hundred yards in front of me. It seemed like I was just slogging along. I held my stance as I rode up the face, counting— *ONE... TWO... THREE... FOUR... FIVE...* — before reaching the top. I had a single quick pause before I was free-falling down the back fifteen to twenty feet, only to see a bigger one behind it. Fearing a wipeout with this looming monster, I repeated the same thing and miraculously was outside the break. After thirty minutes of trying, I was in the clear. I looked around to realize I was alone. There was no helicopter, no sailors, just me.

Sailing alone isn't always the smartest idea, especially in these conditions. But it didn't seem to matter. I felt a sense of calm and peace come over me.

Okay, this is it, I thought to myself. *This is the moment I'm chasing; I'm chasing another opportunity again. And here it is. I'm the only one out, the helicopter is gone, Arnaud isn't around, there are only two or three cars on the point. This is a ridiculous thing that I'm out here.*

But I knew it was going to be okay. I was really in the flow, and it was as if the whole world, my personal reality, just drifted away. These days, we would say I was in the *now*.

I decided the best course of action would be to use the wind squeeze, when a set of four to six waves could give me enough power to skim across the surface.

So off I went. I turned on the last one and sailed toward shore, only to jibe out before it erupted. I would then sail out as another set approached and jibe to sail on the last one again toward shore, turning back to sea before it broke. I repeated this for thirty minutes. I was waiting for something outrageously big, and I had to be ready. I waited for the big wave to show up any minute. Alone out there, my mind was spinning with excitement.

And there it was. I saw my wave standing much taller than anything I had ever seen. I jibed about half a mile in front of it so as to not let it pass me. The apparent winds picked up, and I rode the top of the wave in toward the beach. The winds had turned a little more offshore, so it was difficult to drop straight down the face. I feathered my sail at the top. I looked down into the trough, and it was like I was looking over a six-story building.

This wave was indeed the biggest I had ever seen at Ho'okipa, and I knew I had to get to the bottom quickly. I turned downwind a bit and accelerated down the slope to the trough below. I remember looking up to see the back of the preceding wave—about twenty-five feet tall—when I started losing speed. I tipped my mast forward and opened the sail up to catch the wind, but I kept slowing down. Suddenly, I found myself going backward up the face of the wave I thought I was riding. I couldn't find the wind. I went into irons, and I was in the trough between two waves. The offshore wind was getting blocked by the wave in front.

I was freaking out.

Oh my God, I thought. *This wave hasn't broken yet. I'm afraid to even look up at it because it's about to break.*

I started backing up the face. Now, as it was coming forward, I was going higher and higher backward up the face. I wondered where the lip would hit....

Over me? Under me? THROUGH ME?

Suddenly I felt a giant crash exploding on my tail block behind me, followed by a full whiteout of whitewater. I was inside the whitewater.

I started to loosen my grip on the booms, but I was still standing, so I got a better hold and opened my sail up. Suddenly, I caught a gust of wind, and I was sailing as I came back out of the whitewater.

I guess the air from the collapsing wave pushed me forward. I got a gust of wind that forced me to the beach. Now, this thing was way over my mast. I mean, it might have been a fifty-foot face, and when the waves are that big, the whole reef exposes next to the shore, so I stalled and sailed up the beach.

At Ho'okipa, there's a dirt bank at the back of the beach. I landed about a foot or two from the dirt bank. The wave washed in, pushed me up the beach, and threw me right to the back of Ho'okipa Beach Park. It took me up that far, swirled, and went out, leaving me standing on the sand.

For a minute, I was stunned. I looked around, but I was alone on the beach. It was empty. No one was sailing. Everyone had left.

I had ridden that wave, and it was magnificent, and no one was there to witness it.

Then I heard someone yelling my name.

I turned to see Arnaud running down the bank from the parking lot. He was running full speed with his camera banging against his body.

"Fred! Fred! YOU DID IT! You just rode the biggest wave in the world! This is gonna be huge! This will be much greater than your world record. It's amazing!"

So I hadn't been alone after all. Someone *had* been there to see it. That wonderful, amazing, fantastic friend, Arnaud de Rosnay, was there to see it, helicopter or no.

"I got a full load of film," he said, a big grin on his face. "I took a full roll of film of you on that wave. I've got it!"

In just four months, I had broken a world speed record, and then I rode a big wave—a really big wave.

"You surfed the biggest wave in the world, and you're going to be famous, and this will last longer than your world record. You will be more famous for this than your world record!"

He was absolutely right. Thanks to Arnaud, I was featured—again—in a dozen major magazines, many times on the cover.

"My goodness, Fred, we've never seen a bigger one-two punch in windsurfing," Geoff Cornish, the marketing director at Neil Pryde Sails, said, referring to Weymouth and that day at Ho'okipa. "You're on the team. What do you want?"

That was the ticket I wanted to write. I began earning nearly six figures in the mid-1980s.

I was officially a professional windsurfer.

Ambassadors of Aloha

I n 1985, France held contests within a few months at Saintes Maries de la Mer, Port St. Louis, Fos-sur-Mer, and Gruissan, where the south coast served up heavy winds coming off flat shores and with open fields upwind. So many guys were winning on his boards that Jimmy went over in January before the competitions to shape windsurfing boards for a Paris shop. He was becoming a rock star in Europe.

The four French contests were held about a year after I convinced Laird to move to Maui, where he could get the media attention and sponsorships he deserved. We headed to the south of France to the competition in Port St. Louis. I'd been talking with my sponsor, Neil Pryde Sails, about sponsoring Laird. They were the largest sail builder in the world, and they wanted to say they built the world's fastest sails. I still held the world record from Weymouth. Now Laird had to prove to them that he was fast, and they'd consider taking him on. (It's ironic now to think Laird had to prove himself to anyone. Today, even in his mid-fifties, he is considered the greatest waterman in the world!)

On the final day of the Port St. Louis competition, Pascal Maka was in first place, and Laird was doing okay, but he hadn't placed. He needed to rank in the top three just to get Neil Pryde to pay his expenses for that trip. The whole day the winds were pretty flat, and they halted the contest. Suddenly, in the last hour of the competition, the wind picked up. In typical French style, the officials decided that they would open the course. We all scrambled to the start line to get some runs in while the winds increased.

I had a good feeling about Laird's chances, so I told him to use my rig. I knew it was fast, and with Laird on it, it would be plenty fast.

It was. He made a fabulous run on the best wind and won the contest. He also broke the European speed record and beat Frenchman Pascal Maka on his home turf. Best of all, Neil Pryde Sails awarded Laird Hamilton his first professional sponsorship.

I did a similar thing later in Australia at Fremantle for Anders Bringdal, who was new to speed sailing.

Anders is a speed sailing superstar now—declared the fastest in the world after running the speed canal at the Luderitz Speed Challenge in Namibia. That canal was eight hundred meters, cut through a howling landscape with winds blasting offshore across the beach at sixty knots.

When we met in Maui, Anders was a tall and skinny eighteen-year-old from Sweden, where he raced in light winds on longboards. He was part of the World Cup of windsurfing, which includes racing, wave riding, and the course slalom—not speed sailing. Anders came to Maui in 1986, where he saw his first real wave, meaning the big ones we have on the north shore. I watched him master them pretty quickly—soon, he was sailing up and downwind faster than anyone.

We met at Fremantle, about a half-hour from Perth on the southwest coast of Australia on the Indian Ocean. Anders was sailing for a board manufacturer called Tiga. He wanted to sail in the speed contest—it would be his first race—so Tiga made him a speed board. It was about as thin as a book, and the thing sunk like a rock as soon as he tried to stand on it. I saw what was going on.

"Here, Anders," I said. "I want to ride a ten-meter sail today and smash a record. Take my board."

I was holding a board I had developed and Jimmy had shaped. I wanted to use the larger, ten-meter sail that day, because it would give me the chance to compete in a different class than my usual.

"Cool!" he said.

He put his sail on my board and took it out for a few runs.

Each afternoon there, a sea breeze the Aussies call "the Fremantle Doctor" comes up around one o'clock. I guess they call it "the Doctor" because it cools everything down. It fires up windsurfers because it makes for awesome sailing.

Barry Spanier was with me in Australia for the competition. We had gone to a little food hut up on a hill above the town. We were eating meat pies overlooking the harbor and town when we noticed the Doctor moving in. It looked strong—the wind I'd been waiting for to try out that ten-meter sail. We could see windsurfers starting to sail.

I walked over to a payphone and put in a dime. I called the national television news to let them know that the moment was arriving and that I would be setting a world windsurfing record at Woodman Point, about five miles south of Fremantle. I took any chance I could to promote myself. Good publicity earned me more money from my sponsors. I told the television station I'd be the one with the ten-meter sail with a Neil Pryde logo on it.

Barry and I raced down and got our ten square-meter rig together and onto the water. Minutes later, a helicopter appeared and followed me down the course. That night we were on the news showing the actual run, and the next morning a photo and story were on the front page of the newspaper.

That was the day I rode the big sail and broke a world record. And Anders won the whole contest—his first ever—on my board.

I was as thrilled for Anders as if I'd won that contest myself. I guess the aloha spirit runs deep, no matter how far I travel from Maui.

Traveling to competitions was an event in itself. I often traveled with my Maui windsurfing buddies, including Laird Hamilton, Jimmy Lewis, Erik Beale, Kirk Darrow, Klaus Simmer, and sometimes Mike Waltze, taking a little bit of aloha with us. Jimmy came with me to least a dozen events over the years. If he didn't compete, he sold boards.

Getting our gear there posed a challenge, even in the days before high security and extra checked-baggage fees. We each would have between six and eight board bags, plus support gear likes masts, booms, and harnesses.

Kirk Darrow had a connection with an executive at American Airlines. When we would fly to Europe, we would stay overnight in Dallas. Kirk always brought a bunch of protea flowers and loads of macadamia nuts to give to his friend. She'd upgrade us all to first class and check our mounds of equipment for free. It was a fantastic way to travel, back when travel was fun.

On one trip, Laird and I traveled to Europe, landing at Heathrow in London for a few days on a layover. We didn't have Kirk with us that trip, so we decided to test our charm on our own. We piled all our bags in the center of the baggage area and strolled into the American Airlines office. We asked if we could leave our gear there until we caught our flight home. We offered some goodies from Maui as a sort of peace offering (or bribe?). Laird carried his board bags without wearing a shirt, so he just "happened" to have it off when he walked in. Those women were delighted to store our gear and accepted our tokens of appreciation. They even upgraded our return tickets to first class.

Speed!

By the winter of 1985, everyone was hooking into speed. Weymouth picked up what we were doing on Maui, focusing European eyes on windsurfing. Those guys went crazy for it, and windsurfing speed trials began popping up all over the world.

Back then, we didn't have internet and email to let us know where the contests were. We relied on equipment manufacturers, who sponsored the events, to let us know about them. Barry Spanier and Geoff Bourne of Maui Sails always had the latest news of competitions.

For the next five years, I competed all over the world, in places as diverse as southern France, the Canary Islands, Lethbridge in Canada, and Palm Springs, California. I raced in the ocean, in canals, in retention basins and ditches carved along flat beaches. Where there was both wind and water, somebody figured out a way to speed sail.

Soon, everyone was claiming world records, especially after they could track their speed with a GPS unit in their watch. Someone might be sailing out in the ocean, look down at their wrist, and realize they'd hit thirty-something knots.

"I hit a new world record!" they'd proclaim, with no corroboration whatsoever. They'd call a record for a hundred meters or fifteen meters, even. It got so crazy that Jimmy wrote an article for a windsurfing magazine explaining what categorized a record.

The International Yacht Racing Union established the World Sailing Speed Record Council in 1972 to provide impartial results for all those claims by high-speed sailing craft on water. Only contests of exactly five hundred meters were considered.

If you wanted to sponsor a contest, you had to bring in a committee representative to verify and document the race. That meant you had to have enough money to pay them to stay for as long as it took to get good conditions. Contestants might sit around in hotels for three weeks or longer waiting for the wind.

To an uninformed spectator, a windsurfing speed competition can look like a haphazard free-for-all. Participants don't line up on a starting line waiting for someone to call, "On your mark!" and firing a gun, as they take off in a race to the finish line. No one watches the progress of the runs; spectators and support teams wait at the finish line. If they were to line along the beach, they could block the wind.

Weather conditions vary throughout the day, and a skillful competitor knows how to evaluate the wind. I would sometimes sail twenty or thirty runs throughout the day. At the starting line on each run, a judge would clock my start, and another would be at the finish, five hundred meters down the beach, to mark my time. At the end of the day, whoever sailed the fastest was the winner. You could sail once at noon, clock the fastest time, and win, no matter who sailed the rest of the day.

Skill is essential, of course, and excellent equipment is indispensable. Sometimes good fortune plays a role, as Jimmy Lewis will still assert proudly. Jimmy often competed in professional contests, generally finishing in the middle of the pack. He didn't consider himself particularly competitive. He was the last one to expect that he might beat a world record.

Jimmy went with Erik Beale and me in 1986 to compete in Fuerteventura in the Canary Islands off the coast of Africa. Seven of the top ten contenders were riding his boards, including Pascal Maka, so he was hailed as a celebrity just by showing up.

That day the wind was ferocious—downright scary. If someone fell, it was highly likely a rescue boat couldn't reach them in time. It was so windy we had to walk back up the course—never mind that we might block the wind. When Jimmy took off, he was afraid to hook his harness into his boom. If you fall hard enough in such conditions and cannot release the harness, you can break your back. I had come close to that too many times.

In that single run, Jimmy sailed his best day ever. Hoping just to finish without crashing, he practically flew down the coast at thirty-six knots. He earned third place, the highlight of his professional sailing career. I came in fourth.

I was as thrilled for Jimmy that day as if it had been my victory. We Maui windsurfers had a unique camaraderie, and it was different than just sharing a stoke. We shared a spirit of aloha.

Laird Hamilton describes it as a difference between creative people and competitive people. He says competitive people are fulfilled by winning, and creative people are fulfilled by ideas and accomplishments. Aloha, he says, is a creative philosophy, and it expands as we support each other and share our knowledge.

It is, at its essence, a spirit of generosity.

I agree. I'm not as eloquent as Laird. I say that, in windsurfing, we shared our cheers, and we shared our gear.

Windsurfing was thriving. It was cool to share our knowledge with people we met at contests. We encouraged people around the world to sail faster and better. We didn't consider them to be threats to our success if they learned from us. Perhaps that was because our professional status came not from contest winnings but from sponsors who wanted us to show off their stuff. But Laird says it comes from growing up in Hawaii, where we focus on sharing ideas for what he calls "the interest of the whole."

The Agony of the Ecstasy

n 1986, Kirk Darrow and I went to a contest in Saintes Maries de la Mer. I don't remember if it was January or February, but I do remember it was bitter cold with a blistering wind. When we left our hotel at five-thirty in the morning, a sheet of ice covered the swimming pool. We two Maui boys were not very excited about being on the water in that wind chill.

This particular race was in a canal—a channel twenty meters wide, eight hundred meters long, and one or two meters deep. When we pulled up to the beach in our truck, the winds were pounding at fifty to seventy knots, blowing water right out of the course. We parked facing into the wind to keep it from blowing the truck over—it's happened before!

I had never seen anything like it. It took a while before I could even get up on the board to start down the canal. Whitecaps filled the channel. These winds were so strong, it was scary. I ran halfway down the course at about forty or fifty miles an hour when the course started whiting out, and I hit a big puff. I didn't have enough room to turn. It blew the top of my sail backward, while my board kept traveling forward. The wind carried me upside down in a cartwheel. I could see the beginning of the course while I watched my mast drag in the water. Fortunately, I came out of my harness before I hit the beach, so I didn't break anything.

Kirk took a similar tumble, only worse. The pressure of the wind bent the mast, and he couldn't keep his angle in the course. The wind forced him into a sandbank just fifty feet after he took off. I watched him hit the sand as his board and rig flew a hundred feet into the air, landing five hundred feet away and then cartwheeling down the wet beach. It was ugly.

I experienced an equally frightening day in Australia at the Fremantle contest. The conditions were blazing hot—over a hundred degrees and maybe ninety in the water. I was competing, and when I was about a mile offshore, suddenly the wind died. I was stranded, and it was hot, so I decided to slide into the water. I wrapped my arm across the nose of my board and began a side stroke upwind, hoping to be better positioned for the beach when the wind picked up. All of a sudden, thirty feet in front of me, I saw a shark fin…and then, I didn't. A jolt of fear flooded my nervous system.

Now, I recognize a shark fin when I see one. I never saw many in the waters off Maui, but I had seen a few. Frankly, one is enough. A shark's fin is unmistakable—clearly distinguishable from a dolphin fin—and this one was a foot tall. That meant a fifteen-foot-plus-long shark was beneath that fin.

I know to take a shark seriously. I was horrified, and a little bit in shock. *Where did it go?* I wondered. *Was it beneath me?* I didn't see it swim away.

I managed to slide back up on my board. I lay across my sail. I put one foot on the mast and the other on the tail of my board. I kept one hand on the nose of the board and the other on the boom. With half my body still in the water, my board sunk about six inches below the surface. I lay there motionless like a crab clinging to a rock, with my mind spinning in fear. I don't think I took a breath, that's how scared I was.

At last, another competitor came into view on a big, fat slalom board. I waved him down as frantically as I could without falling off my board.

"Can you just sail back and forth around me for a while?" I asked when he got close. "Because there's a big shark here. I mean, really big."

I hoped this activity might scare away the shark.

He did so for about five minutes. Then, muttering something in an Australian accent with "mate" in it, he took off, leaving me alone to wonder if the shark swam beneath me.

Finally, the wind, the Fremantle Doctor, picked up a bit. I could see white caps forming, and I knew I could reach the shore. I slid gently back into the water and pulled the sail over my head. Holding my boom in one hand and the front of the mast in the other, I performed the most miraculous water start of my life on the tiniest bump of a wave.

When I reached the beach at last, I told the race organizer I had seen a shark—a very, very large shark.

"Oh, mate," he said, "We don't have sharks here. You saw a dolphin!"

He looked at me patronizingly, like I was a dumb American, not an experienced Maui waterman who knew the difference between sharks and dolphins.

The next day at the skippers' meeting, the contest organizers announced that two great white sharks had been spotted a mile offshore. The coast guard called off the competition. I felt vindicated.

The last contest I went to was Fuerteventura.

A Fuerteventura Finish

I n the summer of 1990, I returned to Fuerteventura for a second time. I was at the top of my career. Neil Pryde was paying me a buck or two for every sail sold, and that was putting me close to six figures.

I never dreamed that contest would be my last.

Fuerteventura is one of the Canary Islands in the Atlantic Ocean off North Africa. The island began hosting windsurfing world championships in 1985, a year before Paschal, Eric, Jimmy, and I broke speed records there. Fuerteventura is a world-renowned windsurfing spot, thanks to the funnel of wind that blows along the Sotavento lagoon.

Before I left Maui, I worked with Keith Baxter, who owned Hawaiian Pro Line. He had a machine shop below Barry's sail loft. Sky Kinser and I shaped camber inducers for my sails that would press against the mast and batten in place inside the sail. Cams support the battens to stay the same full shape regardless of how much wind is pushing on them. Camber inducers effectively lock the draft of the sail into one place, keeping the shape of the sail constant, regardless of the airflow. We shaped each cam for a specific spot on the mast so that it would match the curve Barry wanted to see on the sail. We're talking precision craftsmanship for a rig that would allow me to accelerate beautifully in those monster winds off the Sotavento beach.

With the new cams completed, Barry Spanier built a new 4.7 square-meter sail—the cams fit perfectly. With no time to test it, I packed and departed for Fuerteventura.

At Fuerteventura that July 1990, I was winning the speed contest. Suddenly, the winds came up, typical for that part of the world. I was ready. I had Barry's new, tiny sail rig that was good and punchy because the flow was so clean. I took off on a run that felt like it could possibly be a world-record pace.

I was flying. Ahead I noticed a little swell—so subtle, just a few inches were crisscrossing the shoreline. It was just this small mound of water.

All of a sudden, I was upside down, dragging a mast tip along the water. The impact pulled the harness bar through the webbing, broke my mast in half, tore my sail down the middle, and accordioned my booms so they looked like a circle instead of a foil.

I was still hooked in when I came to a complete stop in the water. I heard what sounded like every vertebra from my lower back up to my neck crack at once. The violence of the spill left me in shock. It was pretty scary. I wiggled my fingers and my toes before I moved. Thankfully, they worked.

Okay, I said to myself. *It's okay. Nothing's broken.*

I was in ten inches of water, so I crawled on all fours onto the shore, pulling my equipment along—what was left of it, anyway. When I got out of the water to dry sand, I turned over onto my back and lay there for what seemed like forever, trying to regroup.

My head hurt like hell. But the ocean was a stunning turquoise, and the wind blew its seductive siren song—the best of the day. So I grabbed another rig, got back on my board, and went back out. Thirty minutes later, the wind died. I ended up in fifth or sixth place in the 1990 Fuerteventura Windsurfing World Championship.

My body was bruised, and my pride was a little wounded, but it was my spirit that took the brunt that crash. The feeling was familiar, and within moments, a memory of the Olympic finals in the pool at Long Beach came rushing into my awareness as if it had happened only the day before...

I could hear my dad's voice in the back of my mind:

"Pretty soon, you might find yourself not so excited about it, and you'll want to move on. So move on. That's it. You move away from what you don't want to do."

I was pretty sure I already knew what I wanted to do.

This Excellent Life

I t was a beautiful Saturday in August on Maui, as usual. Most every day is beautiful on Maui. But this day was exceptionally beautiful for me—one I will never forget.

The love of my life and my life partner, Debbie Davis, and I pulled into the parking lot at D.T. Fleming Beach Park on the west side of the island just north of Kapalua and nine miles from Lahaina. The park offers plenty of picnic tables and grass running right up to the half-moon-shaped golden sand beach. It is excellent for bodysurfing, which is why my brother Bill loved it.

Even at nine o'clock in the morning, the beach was crowded with my friends and family who had come to wish a final farewell to my brother, Bill Haywood. It had been just a few weeks since Bill had died, and more than a thousand people (yes, really!) came for a celebration of his life. I knew just about everyone, and I enjoyed a bittersweet but most glorious day as they regaled me with their love for Bill. Everyone had a story to share. Many were touching; others were more than a touch raucous.

In Hawaii, we "talk story." This custom is more than chit-chat. We live on an island, after all, and we observe "island time." Island time has two meanings. One refers to a slowing down, a disregard for the clock. It also means time well spent.

Talking story is an invitation to be fully present, to share a piece of yourself, and invite the other to reciprocate and listen deeply. Sure, it's casual. It's light-hearted. It can border on irreligious. And it is always a generous sharing of experience or memories.

That day my brother Guy and I—the last of the Haywoods—enjoyed talking story with our friends about Bill. We got to hear plenty of memories about our dad and mom, who'd died years earlier. Jim was gone, too, of course, since 1980. Also, our sister Anne had passed on.

The week before, the extended Haywood family held a private service on the water. Until he died, Bill worked for Maui Jim, the iconic sunglasses manufacturer, in their Lahaina corporate office. We all went out on the Maui Jim boat to Molokini crater, a crescent-shaped, partially submerged land mass just off the island. Seven more boats, filled with friends, accompanied our little burial at sea. We scattered Bill's ashes into his beloved Pacific Ocean, floating flower blossoms and leis across the surface, laying him to rest with Mom and Dad, and Jim and Anne. My son Skyler came with his family from New Zealand, and my daughter, Meryl, flew to Maui from Denver. Only my younger son, Evan, in the middle of finals at his private school on the mainland, could not make it. Nevertheless, no matter how many miles might separate us, the Haywood family is virtually inseparable.

That's why, in 1990, I returned from Fuerteventura and made good on my promise to myself to give up competitive speed sailing. I was an older athlete. I had started windsurfing when I was twenty-nine, so ending that career in my late thirties was sensible. My primary sponsor wanted to cut back my commissions, and I was no longer interested in traveling for six months to a year.

Skyler was two years old, Meryl just a toddler. I wanted to watch them grow up.

So I cut a deal with my sponsors for a smaller lump sum of cash, which I used to reestablish my real estate career on Maui. I found I had a knack for finding folks the perfect dream home. I also made a friend with just about every one of them, which is why I treasured Bill's beach party funeral. Friends and family are everything to me—whether I've known them all my life or met them recently when they called looking for real estate.

I certainly appreciated the opportunities my windsurfing career afforded and the support it provided me. As exciting as it was to surf "the biggest wave in the world" and receive the accompanying acclaim, it was soon over. Many have ridden bigger waves. Records will always be broken. Few people remember. The fanfare always dies down. Things pass. I just want to enjoy the ride.

My happiest times during those pioneering windsurfing days were trying new tricks on the water while building better boards with my compadres at Sailboards Maui and discovering the many unknowns of sailing on Maui.

Most of my friends from the early days of Sailboards Maui are still around, and they came to Bill's party. Mike Waltze is making films; the Maui Film Festival recently premiered his film *This Excellent Life* documenting the pioneering days of windsurfing on Maui. Jimmy Lewis is still shaping boards—now kiteboards, stand-up paddleboards, and foil boards, too. BK is a partner in Kaonolua Ranch, a cattle ranch in Kula.

Barry Spanier continues to make sails in Lahaina, now for Trilogy Boats, owned by Randy and Jim Coon's families. I can't wait to go sailing in Barry's new boat being built in California by Berkley Marine Center and with new sails by Art Szpunar at S2 Maui. The "Rosie G" will soon be moored in Lahaina Harbor!

Laird Hamilton will probably turn out to be immortal—even in his fifties, he's looking for ways to be healthier and share his discoveries with the world. I swim regularly with Bill Boyum. Dave Mel, a longtime Maui resident and friend, bought Sailboards Maui and served tourists and windsurfing enthusiasts in Paia until the pandemic closed him up.

Arnaud de Rosnay is gone, but his memory continues to spark affectionate tales among us all.

Mark Spitz couldn't make it to Maui for Bill's celebration, but we enjoyed a long phone conversation after the beach party. Mark shared some hilarious memories about Bill—some I remembered and others I never knew. They all gave me a good laugh.

I shared endorphins with these guys, and we are connected for life—like "blood brothers," as Laird once told me. We all have one thing in common. After three decades of fun on the water, after all these years of making careers and raising families and seeing loved ones leave us, we agree on one thing: "If you're sitting at home, you're not having fun!"

I am fortunate to have grown up on the island of Maui with family and friends who infused me with passion, purpose, and aloha. My dad, Dr. Guy Haywood, was my chief influence, imparting his values in actions, not words. He taught me to do my best, to always be ready to take on what's next, and that collaboration always outdoes competition for life satisfaction.

What does that mean? I took Dad's lessons (and Mom's calm demeanor) and worked them into ideas of my own that have served me well in my life: family and friends come first. Don't take things too seriously. When life offers a detour, take it. Choose curiosity over judgment. Remember that the fanfare always dies down. Share. No matter how rough the wind, there's always a good wave to ride.

Maui also left her profound influence on my life. My pledge, one that I have lived and even incorporated into my business, Fred Haywood Realty, is "Love Life. Live Maui." The spirit of aloha in these Hawaiian Islands is real. It has shaped my life, it has enriched my relationships, and it has informed the way I want to show up in the world. Living on the slope of Haleakala has elevated my perspective and inspired me to lead an extraordinary life. The sacred ocean waters have baptized me in their fierce blessings. Not for a moment do I take for granted the good fortune my life has brought me. For that I am eternally grateful.

Acknowledgments

I am very grateful for the many friends who inspired and motivated me along my forty-year sport and adventure journey to create this memoir.

My brother, Guy Haywood, gave me great insights into Maui and our family experience. I look forward to our Pirates' Christmas dinner on our view deck in Kula with all my wonderful relatives, whom I love dearly but didn't mention in this book.

Many thanks to Mark Spitz, Jim Gaughran, John Ferris, Rick Eagleston, Herbert Mason, Mitch Ivey, Ted Nichols, Brent Berk, Mike Waltze, Bill and Peggy King, Barry and Samantha Spanier, Geoffrey and Debbie Bourne, Demitri Milovich, Sky Kinser, Jimmy Lewis, Laird Hamilton, Kai Lenny, Dana Dawes, Lena Kerr, Shirley Randall, Joyce Dottavio, Kelby Anno-Bruno, Rhonda Smith-Sanchez, Ken Kleid, Jonathan Weston, Robbie Naish, Peter Cabrinha, Josh and Amy Stone, Bill Boyum, Vince Hogan, Mark Paul, Scotty O'Conner, Peter Boyd, Shawn Conners, Barkley Bastian, Doug Hunt, Paul Ehman, Lenny Cappe, Craig Maisonville, Alex and Greg Aguera, Malta and Klaus Simmer, David Ezzy, Jeff Hendersen, Rob and Ginny Karpovitch, Rob and Margaret Kaplan, Matt and Shawneen Schweitzer, Hoyle and Diane Schweitzer, Martin and Paula Lenny, Robert and Mary Jo Masters, Erik and Bonnie Aeder, Steve Wilkings, Darrel Wong, Keith and

Karen Baxter, Pascal Maka, Anders Bringdal, Bjorn Dunkerbeck, Ken Winner, Robert Teritehau, Erik Beale, Alan and Patti Cadiz, Dave and Mariko Mel, Victor and Gerry Lopez, Jeff Hakman, Bernie Baker, Jack McCoy, Kim von Tempsky, Larry and Ceci Gilbert, Peter and Becca Kalina, Rob and Luanne Yapp, Mark Brown, Dano Sayles, Dino Cordova, George Martin, Steven Mangum, Matt Dickey, Mama's Fish House, Maui Jim Sunglasses, and Fred Haywood Realty.

Thank you to all the Maui friends and families who touched my life and to the many swimmers, surfers, and windsurfers whom I have had the privilege to meet and share wonderful experiences around the world as well as here, in and off the waters of Maui!

A special thank you to my life partner, Debbie Davis, who, through her love and encouragement, helped in every way possible to make the book a reality and my life better than ever while being adored and loved by my children. Skyler Haywood, my oldest son, now lives in New Zealand with his wife, Suzie, and my granddaughter Gwendoline. In addition to managing an Air New Zealand VIP lounge in Plymouth, Skyler and Suzie share a passion to surf, windsurf, and foil every day they can. Meryl Haywood, my daughter, is using her years of art study in Florence, Italy, in finding her passion as a hairstylist in Denver, Colorado. Evan Haywood, my younger son, is attending Besant Hill School in California, dreaming of a good college at the end of next year. Evan is at an exciting age while finishing his education.

A big *mahalo* to my friend and literary agent, Michael Ebeling, who introduced me to David Hancock of Morgan James Publishing. Their enthusiasm for my journey, as told in these pages, delights me.

Lastly, I would like to acknowledge my collaborative writer, Donna Mosher, who motivated me through her compassion, perseverance, and great talents to make this book a reality. I am forever grateful to Donna!

Maui is and always will be a wonderful place, and with tourism, it is important for everyone to show respect for the *'aina*, culture, people, and visitors alike. The Maui waterfalls and pools are still flowing, the sunrises and sunsets remain magical, the beaches are still pristine, and the air is clean with the sugar cane burning gone, so we just have to learn to share this Maui experience with more people coming this way. *Maui no ka oi* and *mahalo nui loa*!

About the Author

Fred Haywood was born on the island of Maui a decade before it became a state. The son of a sugar plantation doctor, he grew up playing with the neighbor kids, who were Hawaiian, Japanese, Chinese, and white. Fred and his four siblings played in the waters off Kahului Harbor on balsawood surfboards and El Toro sailboats. He and his buddies trekked around the island, surfing, camping, and diving for fish from Honolua Bay to Hana.

When Fred was sixteen, he left home to join George Haines's world-famous Santa Clara swim team. A year later, he and Mark Spitz were the first high school students to win the National Championships in Dallas, Texas, and Fred became the fastest backstroker in America. Fred was a silver medalist at the 1967 Pan American Games and became a multiple NCAA and American record holder. He went on to swim for Jim Gaughran at Stanford University, where he became the swim team captain.

Fred continued his winning ways when, in 1983, he broke the world speed record in Weymouth, England, to become the fastest windsurfer in the world, a record he held for two years.

Fred Haywood excelled in windsurfing competitions until, at the practically ancient age of forty, he gave up his professional sports career to raise a family and sell real estate on his beloved Maui. He is now one of the most successful realtors on the island and a popular teacher for realtors around the country.

CPSIA information can be obtained
at www.ICGtesting.com
Printed in the USA
JSHW022339230721
17201JS00002B/3

9 781631 953712